BEHOLD!
GOD IS SPEAKING TO US

XULON PRESS

BEHOLD!

GOD IS SPEAKING TO US

A Fifty-two Week Old Testament Devotional

MICHELLE GEHRT

XULON PRESS

Xulon Press
2301 Lucien Way #415
Maitland, FL 32751
407.339.4217
www.xulonpress.com

© 2019 by Michelle Gehrt

Unless otherwise indicated, Scripture quotations taken
from the New King James Version (NKJV). Copyright
© 1982 by Thomas Nelson, Inc. Used by permission.
All rights reserved.

Printed in the United States of America.

ISBN-13: 978-1-5456-6331-8

"In order to better know the new, we must also be friends with the old! Michelle Gehrt has just written THE go-to devotional for those seeking a deeper application of how Old Testament scripture is very much relevant still today. Read this weekly devotional… and let <u>Behold Moments; How God Speaks to Us!</u> be the tool to better build your Christian vocabulary!»
— *Scott McCallum, cofounder of "The Share Mission" (<u>www.TheShareMission.com</u>).*

Have you ever wondered if the Old Testament could have any significant impact on your 21st century life? I know I have. Consider this your invitation to take a close look at the lives of these esteemed, yet fallible saints of old. You will be assured of God's unfailing love and faithfulness, and gain a renewed sense of Christ in me; the hope of glory!
— *Janice Craycroft, Associate Director of Victory Ministries Center of Hope*

FOREWORD

That the God of creation wants to speak to us and through us is amazing to think about. Yet here in Michelle's devotional, the reader encounters that awesome miracle at work. *Behold!* is a prophetic devotional birthed from prophetic activation. This devotional is Romans 11:36 in real life—"For of Him and through Him and to Him are all things to whom be glory forever." Because this devotional was birthed from His heart for the reader, it came about through His power at work in Michelle's obedience, and because she offers it back to Him for His glory, *Behold!* will impact many lives. Those lives will be transformed into His image and therefore, His kingdom will be advanced. "You are worthy, O Lord, to receive glory and honor and power; For You created all things, and by Your will they exist and were created."

—Betty Kulich, Assoc. Pastor
Redeemer's Church, Columbus, Ohio

Acknowledgments

My Father in heaven for using me as a vessel to help others.

The Holy Spirit for guiding me, giving me the words for each devotional and speaking through me.

My husband Jim without whom I could have never written this book if it hadn't been for his support, encouragement along the way, listening to the devotionals, having faith in me, and pushing me forward as the struggle was real at times. I love you!

My children, for being sounding boards, being patient with me and encouraging me. I love you guys!

My Aunt Pam, for new ideas and ways of thinking differently. Thank you for believing in me.

Family support.

Denise and Georgia for encouraging me to write this devotional. Thank you for your continual support and guidance my missionary friends!

Pastor Betty Kulich from Redeemers Church for being a soundboard, reading and writing the foreword for my book and for having Godly wisdom and scriptural insight when I needed it.

Janice Craycroft with Victory Ministries Center Of Hope, thank you for believing in this project; spending the time to comb through my manuscript and being a great friend!

Scott McCallum with The Share Mission, thank you for always being there for me and being a constant friend through the years. I am thankful for your support.

The scripture Phil gave me prophetically at Redeemers Church Prophetic School.

The pens given to me by my friends Paul and Martha at Redeemers Church Prophetic School to begin my book. Thank you, Holy Spirit for using them!

Tana, who encouraged me to keep pushing and not to second-guess what God was doing. Thank you for keeping me on track.

Alecia for taking this journey with me and supporting me faithfully through all the twists and turns. I am thankful for you!

All my friends for, their loving unconditional support through the process.

DEDICATION

For Vincent, Dominik, Isabella, and Michael. May this book inspire you to take bold steps of faith in life. Anything is possible with God on your side. He holds your life in His hands, and He has purposed your lives for more than you could ever imagine.

I love you all,
Mom

INTRODUCTION

The inspiration for writing this book comes from a yearning within my spirit to show the love of the Lord through encouraging words and Bible verses. This material can be used to think about on a weekly basis, showing you how God has purposed your life and how to live through the Holy Spirit within you,

I had been hearing the word *behold* for months, but I never thought anything of it. I finally realized that "behold," meant something when I was prophetically given the scripture Isaiah 43:18–19. This verse inspired my book. I realized that God is doing something new just as the scripture says. I knew that I was to share the Father's declarations in the Bible of what His Words say to give strength, hope, faith, and encouragement that can only come from Him. He loves us as we are. Through all of the ways that God was speaking to me about the word *behold* and through the help of the Holy Spirit, I began to write this devotional. I put a lot of my time into this book by praying to God that I could be a vessel used by Him to get the scriptures from the Bible that He wanted me to use to show us how much He loves us and will never leave us.

As you read through this devotional one week at a time; pray, reflect, meditate, and journal your thoughts. Invite God to take this journey with you. Ask the Holy Spirit to open your eyes, ears, and heart to guide you. Listen for the still, small voice of the Lord.

My prayer is that this book inspires, encourages, and strengthens the mind, body, soul, and spirit. I pray that this book gives confirmation to know who we are in the Lord and to know that we were bought for a price to do kingdom work for the glory of the Lord. May our Father in heaven use this book to unveil eyes and transform the minds of His sons and daughters. I pray that whoever reads this book receives what the Holy Spirit is doing within them and all eyes are open. May the Holy Spirit guide and direct paths, and may all become refreshed and renewed, ready to begin the day with all of the wonderful possibilities that God has breathed within them.

Come, Holy Spirit, have your way with us.

CONTENTS

Week 1

HOPE

*Do not remember the former things, nor
consider the things of old. Behold, I will
do a new thing, Now it shall spring forth;
Shall you not know it? I will even make
a road in the wilderness and rivers in
the desert. (Isaiah 43:18–19 NKJV)*

Behold! He is doing a new thing.

The word *behold* is not an ordinary word. It is a strong word that makes you think about its meaning when you come upon it. The Oxford English Dictionary definition of the word behold is, to look upon a thing or a person, especially a remarkable or impressive one. Biblegateway. com shows that the word behold appears 1298 times in the original King James Version (published in the 1600s).

Behold! Look and see the Spirit within you. God is doing new things in your life continually. Don't rely on what once was, but look to what God is doing now, today at this present moment. You are special, and you were created to be unique in all of your ways. The Lord has purposed gifts within you from the beginning. In Psalm 139:13–16, David proclaims that God's eyes were fixed on you before you were even born. You were made from nothing into something. He watched you from conception to birth and until your last breath on earth. He loves you in all your ways. Your uniqueness is what sets you apart from each other.

The Lord has deposited favor in you, that makes you who you are. He has a plan for your life and has prepared the way for you. Finding and learning your gifts will give you wisdom and discernment to live out your calling here on earth. This precious package that has been designed within you from our Lord will help you grow the more you search out your gifts. These gifts will provide clarity, guidance, and discernment that can only come from the Holy Spirit within. You were made for more! You are sons and daughters of the Most High. You are equipped with how to live each day because God is always doing something new within you. He loves you so much that His only begotten Son went to the cross for you to live. He bore His stripes to save you. When you ask for forgiveness, you invoke the power of the Holy Spirit and you no longer have to feel you are a slave to sin. What was in the past is gone and forgiven. Now is the time to look to what God is doing new in you.

Behold, He is doing a new thing!

Week 2

IN THE WAITING

Then I will give them a heart to know Me, that I am the Lord; and they shall be My people, and I will be their God, for they shall return to Me with their whole heart. (Jeremiah 24:7 NKJV)

Behold! He is with you always and will never leave you behind.

God desperately wants us. He wants us to know Him. He wants us to know what it is to let Him guide us and to be used by Him. He is a forgiving Father. He is the only one who can give us grace, and He proves it time and time again throughout the Bible. He is with us always through the roller-coaster journey of life. He allows us choice because He wants us to want Him. Our choices allow us to learn in life and to know that without Him, we are nothing.

When we give our lives to God, a veil is torn, and our eyes are fresh new eyes, just like seeing through a baby's eyes. Finally we can begin our true journey here on earth. We can use our gifts to do our assignments that God has waiting for us. Our Father is unchangeable, everlasting, and faithful. He is true to His promises and is willing and able to perform for us. He is on our side. We may fall backward in life, but through repenting, we will return to the Father just as the prodigal son did.

He is always in the waiting, in the stillness. He is that small breathe of fresh air and the wind in our lungs. He is in our thoughts and is there through our convictions; whispering "I am here and I love you; turn back to me and experience all I have to offer for you. You are my sons and daughters." Our Father teaches us love through the Holy Spirit within us. He shows us this when we step outside of ourselves to love one another. He cares for us and brings people and things to us when we are in need. These are not coincidences; this is God doing the miraculous in your life. You have an earthly father, but God is our heavenly Father. He knew us in the womb before we were born, and He continues to fight for us each day. He is our strength when we are weak and our rock when we need a firm foundation. He is here right now, today and for always. Open your eyes and see the beauty all around you. Seek Him by reading His Word each day. Pray to Him like you are having a regular conversation, and thank Him for saving you and being a good, good Father.

Behold! He is with you always and will never leave you behind because He keeps all of His sheep together. He is the good Shepherd, and He has the living water that we thirst for. Reach out to Him and learn today that the Holy Spirit within you is your lamp on your journey. He will keep it bright when you choose to let go of control and life's grips. Hang on to your Father in heaven.

Week 3

SUPREMACY

And when he saw that, he arose and ran for his life, and went to Beersheba, which belongs to Judah, and left his servant there. (1 Kings19:3 NKJV)

Behold! You are never alone. He has a plan and purpose for your life. Listen for His voice.

Are you overwhelmed? Do you feel discouraged or maybe fearful? Do you feel helpless or defeated? Elijah, in the book of 1 Kings, felt all of these things at once. In fact his mental stability during that time was wavering. Elijah's calling from God had a purpose and a plan: to anoint two kings and pass his prophetic gifting on to his assistant Elisha (1 Kings19:15–16 NKJV).

Elijah allowed negative emotions he was experiencing to impact his calling from God. He was concerned with all of the circumstances, rather than looking at the center of what was going on. It is easy to get caught up in life's junk. We all do it from time to time. Elijah was so overwhelmed and filled with fear that he went on the run. While he was running away, God's presence was still with him just like God's presence is with you today.

You may be going through junk and may be surrounded by so many problems that you cannot see that God is there and has a plan and purpose for you. It took Elijah to end up in a cave to hear the still, small voice of God. We cannot hear God when we are surrounded by commotion, confusion, and negativity. No wonder why Elijah ran off. He was the last prophet left and had no one to rely on or speak to. At that time, there was mass confusion and terrible things happening in the Northern Kingdom because of a terrible king. In 1 Kings 19:11–13, God was making a way for His presence to be heard through Elijah in the cave. He was going through all kinds of turmoil, and God first produced a strong wind, then an earthquake, and finally a fire. God was not in any of these forces of nature, but what followed was the grace of God and His comforting voice speaking to Elijah. What are you afraid of? God is in control of all things. Even when we can't see what lies ahead, we must rely on the promises of God in scripture and through faith that God has marked our path and has a plan for our lives.

Behold! Do not fear; you are never alone. He is the Cup you drink from that gives you everlasting life in Him. Through life struggles, remember your Father and listen for His loving voice. His presence is with you and always goes with you because you are His child. Pray and open your eyes to see the powerful hand of God.

Week 4

PROMISES

Come now, therefore, and I will send you to Pharaoh that you may bring My people, the children of Israel, out of Egypt. (Exodus 3:10 NKJV)

Behold! God's promises hold true! Just as he was with Moses, He is with you.

In Exodus 3, God called Moses to do the unthinkable. He heard the cries of His children in Egypt in slavery. The cries made Him remember His covenant that He made with Abraham, Isaac, and Jacob. That promise was that Abraham would have so many descendants as he could count the stars in the sky. He was going to get them out of bondage to keep His promise, and He chose Moses to do this. Can you imagine how Moses felt? He was a shepherd in the land of Midian, married with a son. All of a sudden, Moses is approached by the Angel of the Lord in the desert at a mountain in a burning bush that really was not being burnt up. When Moses decided to take a look at the bush, God called Moses by his name. When Moses understood it was God, he was scared. Can you imagine all the emotions Moses was feeling? God told Moses that He would send him to bring His people out of Egypt. What a great responsibility God had placed on Moses.

Has someone ever asked you to do something that was so big that you were scared of not being able to do it or even wonder why you were asked to do it? Did you wonder if you were not good enough or maybe others would not believe you because you did not have all the answers? Have you ever thought you weren't qualified? God does not care if you are not qualified for the assignment. He will equip you when He calls you. He is prepping you for other things when you obey Him. God knows your heart and all of your inner workings. Don't let your emotions get into the way of what God wants to do through you. When God opens a door for you, walk through it with faith and hope. He is taking you on a journey that is paving your life purpose to many other things. He is preparing you for the next greatest thing.

God was preparing Moses to be a prophet and to speak His law to the people. All of this happened after Moses delivered God's children by being obedient, even though he may have been unsure at times. God knows you inside out and is calling on you to do many things that will strengthen your walk with Him through obedience to say yes. The next time you are feeling like you're not good enough or question your way, pray to your Father and remember what He did through Moses. He will direct all of your ways.

Behold! God's promises hold true. He is with you just as He was with Moses.

Week 5

CHOSEN

"You are My witnesses," says the Lord,
"And My servant whom I have chosen,
That you may know and believe Me,
And understand that I am He. Before
Me there was no God formed, Nor shall
there be after Me." (Isaiah 43:10 NKJV)

Behold! You have been chosen by God your Father to testify who He is and to be an example for all to see. You have been handpicked to be the vessel that the Lord wants to use for His glory!

A witness is someone who provides evidence of what he or she proclaims to know about a matter (Merriam-Webster Dictionary). Just as Jesus ministered to the disciples, showing them His great acts and teaching them by His Words, you are witnesses to what the Lord has done in and through you. Through consistent time in prayer and through reading scripture, your walk with

God will increase beyond knowledge, and you will become a forerunner for God. Your assignment is to take your life and make it a testimony for someone else to hear to bring them to the Father, just as you have come to know Him.

Jesus was a chosen servant from the Lord, called for a purpose on a mission for God. The Lord wants to do great things through you. He does not care about your former life; He cares that you know who you are in Him. He wants you to help Him gather His harvest and return the lost, broken, and helpless to Him. He wants the Holy Spirit's light within you to radiate His presence within you for all to see. He chose you!

The Lord wants you to trust in Him in all circumstances. He tells us in Isaiah 43:10 that there is no God before Him, and there will be none after Him. This is proof of the Father showing you He is omnipotent and omnipresent. He has the last word! This life may cause pain, but He is there, and through the trials of life you are strengthened in Him. There is only one way to the Father, and that is through His only begotten son, Jesus. Choose to believe!

Behold! You are a chosen one to be a witness to Him and to spread His story, walking by faith, not by sight. You are a warrior; a watchman by day and night, making sure that all who encounter your presence will see the essence of the Father's love.

Week 6

PERSISTENCE

Now Hannah spoke in her heart; only
her lips moved, but her voice was not
heard. (1 Samuel 1:13 NKJV)

Behold! The Lord will always remember you.
Hannah was persistent in her prayer life. Hannah
prayed from what her heart desired most. She was unable
to have children, and through her fervent prayers to the
Lord, she made a vow to the Lord that if He gave her a
child, she would dedicate the child to the service of the
Lord for all of his days. It seems as if Hannah was at wits
end. In those days, it was a shame for a wife not to be
able to bear children, and Hannah was often provoked
because of this. Put yourself in Hannah's shoes for a
moment. How would you react in this situation? What
would you do?

Can you imagine praying to God and telling Him
that if He helped you to conceive that you would give

your child back to Him? Hannah had nothing left but her prayer to the Father. She was constant in her prayers and knew that if God would remember her, then she would do the unthinkable. She was a woman of faith and courage. She realized that everything good comes from up above. Samuel was a blessing to Hannah, and she was gracious that God came through. She dedicated Samuel to the Lord, and the Lord blessed her with three more sons and two daughters.

This story of hope and truth shows us that God is always listening to us. He knows what we need. Hannah was desperate and full of grief, and God remembered Hannah. This shows us the heart of God. Samuel was a great accomplishment to God. Samuel came on God's timing, and God has purposed his every step. God was always working in Hannah's life, just as He is working in your life today. Sometimes we do not understand why things are the way they are or why events happen in a certain manner, but God does. He has a plan and purpose for every waking moment of your life. Hannah trusted God, even though she could not see the light in her story. Do you trust God in all areas of your life? Can you stand upon the promises of God even when you're in the rain? Can you be content in the struggle?

Behold! The Lord will never forget you. He is with you in times of distress.

Week 7

TRUST

If that is the case, our God whom we serve is able to deliver us from the fiery furnace, and He will deliver us from your hand, O king. But if not, let it be known to you O king, that we do not serve your god's, nor will we worship the gold image which you have set up. (Daniel 3:17–18 NKJV)

Behold! Trust in the Lord your God. He is able and willing. He has done it before and will do it again. He always comes through.

Trust is the word we think of when we see what was happening to Daniel and his friends. You see Daniel and his friends were just youths approximately fifteen years old when they were handpicked, chosen as slaves to go to Babylonia and serve under a ruthless king. They were to forget their old life and adapt a new life of the Chaldeans. They had to change their names, which were all godly, honorable names to now honor the Babylonian gods, with their language, customs, and diet. They were not allowed to pray to their God. Can you imagine being a child, torn from your family, put into a new culture, and having to forget who you were or where you came from?

Daniel and his friends did as they were told and learned the language and customs of the Babylonians. Just because they were forced to change stuff on the outside, they knew who their God was in their hearts, and they chose to obey Him in this situation. They would not bow down to the king's idols because they trusted that their God would be with them and knew He was the only everlasting God, true to His promises.

Daniel's friends were thrown into a fiery furnace for not worshipping the king's idols. When they were thrown in, they told the king that their God is able to deliver them and even if He chose not to, they would still not bow to their idols (Daniel 3:17–18 NKJV). A miracle was performed that day. The unthinkable happened. Daniel's friends were not the only ones in the fiery furnace, but the Son of God was in there with them, preserving them from harm! The king was amazed and told the kingdom that no one was to say a word against their God. Daniel and his friends trusted God in their situation. After reading the story of Daniel, it makes you see that with having trust in the Lord your God, the unimaginable will happen. In your season of uncertainty, look to the book of Daniel and reflect on the goodness of our Father.

Behold! Even in the fire, God is at work in your lowest time! Trust in Him.

Week 8

FIRST FRUITS

This book of the law shall not depart from your mouth, but you shall meditate in it day and night, that you may observe to do according to all that is written in it. For then you will make your way prosperous, and then you will have good success. (Joshua 1:8 NKJV)

B ehold! Give God the first fruits of your day; then watch and see what He does for you.

When we choose to give the first of our day to God by opening up our Bibles and soaking in His Word, we are becoming spiritually disciplined, and slowly we will begin to see things differently. Our minds will become transformed into His image. Our thoughts will flow differently. The words we speak from our tongue will at first seem foreign to us but will slowly begin to flow like milk. Reading from the Word will not only give us insight into our lives, but we will gain great wisdom and strength for the days to come. His love, teachings, and correction in our lives have no boundaries.

Anything that we could ever want to know about is in the Bible. Scripture reveals that God brings comfort, strength, encouragement, belief, wisdom, discernment, forgiveness, and more. Reading scripture and meditating on what God is showing us allows us to live by what His Word says. It allows us to take captive anything that is not spoken of God. We gain everlasting faith and trust in who God says He is and what He is doing. We learn what our gifts are and how God wants to use us for His coming kingdom. Through God's declarations, we see how He is moving through our lives. He provides everything we could ever need, and it is written in the scriptures. We learn that God has paved our path, and His Spirit within us is the light at our feet as we walk. We begin to realize that without God in our lives, we are nothing.

Being sons and daughters calls for great strength here on earth, and it can only come with a firm foundation and relationship with our Father. The only way to know Him is through prayer and to know who he is through His written Word. We are here for a purpose that is greater than our minds can perceive. We have been chosen and handpicked to come here for His works and great glory. We are called to be vessels for Him to be used by Him to bring others into unity with our Father in heaven. We have been picked by our

Father to guide others to know who He is and to bring them into a life of everlasting love and wellness. This can't happen unless we know who He is to us and what His Word says.

Behold! Give God your first fruits and watch and see what He has in store for your day!

Week 9

CONSTANT

Therefore know that the Lord your God, He is God, the faithful God who keeps covenant and mercy for a thousand generations with those who love Him and keep His commandments. (Deuteronomy 7:9 NKJV)

B ehold! He is our constant. Lord, help us be more like you.

God never changes, but we change. We change as the wind changes. One day we like something, and the next we don't. Does our word at times even mean anything? God's word is His Word. He is our constant. He is our stability. He is our security and our safety net. He carries us and walks with us. His Word is written in and on us. He loves us, and He waits on us. His presence is with us always, and He knows our every thought—good or bad. He is the Great I Am. We are His children, and

He is our Father. We will never be higher than Him, but we can be like Him, which is the best way to be! When we stand on His firm foundation, His light is a beacon that shines through us for all to see.

Throughout life, we recognize that someone or something will always fail us. How wonderful it is to know that our God will never fail us! He is ever present and willing to listen to us. When we enter a time of prayer with Him, we open ourselves up to desperately wanting and needing Him. He is in the waiting for us. He is everywhere. God is constantly talking to us. We need to tune into what God is saying. Psalm 46:10 says, "Be still and know that I am God." It is in the stillness that we can hear our Father. God speaks to us through our thoughts. It is through our spirit that we communicate with God. When you seek God, He will respond by putting His wants into your heart. He will show you that He is constant, never changing, and always here for you. God's love is unconditional. His promises last forever. Doesn't that feel good to know that the Lord is always on your side and is fighting for us?

Deuteronomy 7:9 tells us to turn to Him because He is faithful. We can always put all of our trust in Him. There will be times of uncertainty in our lives, and when these times come, we can rest assured that we have a loving Father in heaven, who is constant and faithful that we can call out to. Come, Holy Spirit, fill our mind with your faithfulness. Increase our trust in You, Father. Help us; Father, to be more like you.

Behold! He is faithful! Put your trust in Him and watch how He strengthens you for each day.

Week 10

HUMILITY

But truly I am full of power by the Spirit of the Lord, And of justice and might, To declare to Jacob his transgression And to Israel his sin. (Micah 3:8 NKJV)

Behold! As believers, we have the gift of the Holy Spirit within us to help guide us and transform our thoughts, giving us a spirit of humility, shedding light on seeing things with new eyes.

How well do you respond to criticism or correction? Do you get mad, or maybe you feel like no one understands you at times because you feel as if they are always trying to bring you down? Micah, a minor prophet and a contemporary of the prophet Isaiah, had to give a message to leaders of both the Northern and Southern Kingdoms of Israel. This message could be seen from the leaders as a message of warning, love, and new ways to become what the Lord has purposed them to be. God used Micah to make things right.

Micah, whose name means "Who is like the Lord," was called to be a mouthpiece for God. God's hand was on Micah in this time, and his strength came from the Lord. God used Micah to warn Israel of all of their idolatries and more. Micah was full of God's power. The Spirit of the Lord was in and with him. In the Old Testament, the Holy Spirit did not play the same role as in the present day. The Holy Spirit today lives in all who believe. Micah was obedient to take the Lord's assignment.

It takes a lot of humility to take any kind of correction. I think we all can agree that it is hard when someone does not agree with us for different reasons. Sometimes, we feel as if we are not being heard or that no one understands us. At times, it's tough to see that a loved one is being true because they love us. The hope is to be able to take what they say into consideration and take a step back and rethink what we are saying or doing. We can look at those as trying to help us see things differently. We can view this as the idea that God sent them to us to guide us into slowly shifting and transforming us into what God intends for us. Micah was sent to warn the kingdoms, to save them from what was about to happen. The next time you encounter correction of any kind, try not to take it personally and separate your emotions from your thoughts. Try to see what they are saying to you, so you can see things with fresh eyes.

HUMILITY

Behold! God is using others to help humble us and to show us new ways at looking at things!

Week 11

BEAUTY FOR ASHES

"To console those who mourn in Zion, To give them beauty for ashes, The oil of joy for the morning, The garment of praise for the spirit of heaviness; That they may be called trees of righteousness, The planting of the Lord, that He may be glorified." (Isaiah 61:3 NKJV)

Behold! We are surrounded by our Father! This is how we fight our battles!

How do you fight your battles when you have been utterly broken time and time again in life? How do you get back up and do it again? Isaiah 61:3, is a beautiful picture of beauty for ashes. The beauty, that comes from brokenness in life. Sadness is replaced by joy when we learn to put on the garment of praise in and through our struggle. In our weakness, it is God's strength that gets us through. Have you turned away from God during this time, thinking He is not present? This is what the Israelites did in this time period. They would follow God and obey the covenant and then turn away from God.

God knows that this life will bring trials and tribulations. He wants us to stick close to Him during the good and bad times of life. That is what faith is. Is it hard to do? Depending on what hurt, pain, or struggle you're going through, it can be extremely hard to see past the situation you're currently in. The challenges you face will strengthen you and increase your dependence on the Lord. To get past the ashes on your life journey, rejoice and praise Him. Praising the Lord brings healing from all suffering. This is where your beauty comes from. God's glory radiates in the beauty.

Come to the Father with your suffering. He is the great Comforter. Pray to Him and ask Him to heal you and strengthen you for all your days to come. Ask Him to show you how you can use your struggle to help someone else. Your ashes are part of your story. Your testimony is meant to be shared to show others what type of freedom comes from a loving relationship with Jesus Christ. The words you give to others will transform many lives, bringing them into a deeper foundation in the Lord. This foundation will create a "new" relationship in Him and will begin to take deep roots. How rooted are you in the Lord in tough times? Will you avoid His promises, or will you hold steadfast through the ashes to see the beauty in the morning?

Behold! When you are suffering, put on the garment of praise. Lean on your Father in the ashes, and you will begin to see the beauty. God has a plan for your life. You were made for more.

Week 12

SEEK HIS FACE

"Seek the Lord and His strength; Seek His face evermore!" (1 Chronicles 16:11 NKJV)

Behold! Never stop searching for the Lord!

How is your relationship with God? How is your relationship with Him when you feel lost in life? What about when life has you at a halt? Maybe your life is going fantastic, and you're pushing forward, anticipating what tomorrow will bring. How is your relationship with God in the good times? It's never too late to start living each day for God. He loves you and is always with you.

Correlating 1 Chronicles and 2 Samuel 6:16, the Ark of the Covenant was being carried to the city of King David. David was so excited that he was singing, dancing, and leaping for joy. His song was one of thanksgiving and praise. The Ark of the Covenant was a manifestation of God's presence, and it was being brought to David! Can you imagine this joy! This is what today's verse is all about. We are to continually look high and low for God's face. We are to pursue God at all costs because only He can comfort us and give us peace. His presence goes with us always, and that is why it's important to encounter God through a personal relationship with Him.

God is with us, the same way that God was with Israel. Just like a child, a son or daughter who may not listen or make wrong choices against their father, Israel also did that, and we do it, too. The gift is that God is merciful and gives us grace beyond what we deserve or can even imagine. He is with us when we make wrong turns in life, just as He is there when we are on the right path. He is there in sickness and health, for rich or poor, and when we are broken and lost. His presence goes with us always. Have you made the choice to receive the Lord? If you have not yet, you can right now, by asking God for forgiveness for your sins and telling the Lord that you want to live a life through Jesus Christ. The next step is to receive Him through baptism so that you can die to your old life, rise with your Father in heaven, and become a new creation.

Behold! He loves you so much and is jealous for all of you. Don't stop searching Him out.

Week 13

GIFTINGS

For behold, you shall conceive and bear a son. And no razor shall come upon his head, for the child shall be a Nazirite to God from the womb; and he shall begin to deliver Israel out of the hands of the Philistines. (Judges 13:5 NKJV)

B ehold! Nothing blocks God from doing His will! He is the everlasting Father who loves you.

The story of Sampson and Delilah is a story of sin and being spiritually blind due to obsession. Delilah got Sampson to tell her the secret of his strength in Judges 16:1–31, which led him to his death. God gifted Sampson with supernatural strength, but he got sidetracked. God had a purpose and plan for Sampson, and he chose to listen to a Philistine woman rather than stay obedient to God. His love for her led Sampson to do things that changed the course of his entire life. God had a purpose and plan for Sampson, as He does for you. It is easy to veer off course when someone talks you into believing or doing something that is not right. Has anyone ever said something to you that you knew was not right, and because of not wanting to be uncomfortable or embarrassed, you made a bad decision? Sampson knew the right thing to do, but he allowed obsession to take over. He had a thing for Philistine women. He chose Delilah over God's declaration for his life. He did not want to lose what he thought was good. Instead of being obedient to what was spoken over him, he chose to veer off God's chosen path. By taking a different path, he missed out on glorifying God. By the time Sampson died, he had judged Israel for over twenty years. God still loved Sampson and gave him grace.

Rejection is tough. We are humans in an earthly world, and it's hard to grasp that our Father is heavenly and is here on earth, guiding us through His Spirit in this time. We don't want to be cast out or left alone, which leads us to becoming blind to what is right in front of our face. We can't allow our emotions to get in the way of what God wants to do in and through us. Maybe you're a writer or have the gift of music, love to help others, teach, or are a good listener. Maybe you're an encourager or have the gift of prayer. Regardless, don't allow others to cause you to step outside of your gifting. We all have gifts God has given to us. Whatever gift you have been given is unique for you and your calling here on earth. Your gift will shine through you when you start using it. Do you know your gifts? Sampson's gift was his strength. What is yours?

Behold! Pray earnestly to the Father and seek Him continually to reveal what He has for you.

Week 14

SEASONS

To everything there is a season, a time for every purpose under heaven: (Ecclesiastes 3:1 NKJV)

B ehold! The power of God has divinely appointed this season under heaven. Only God knows what season you are in. Praise Him in this time!

What season are you in right now? Did you know that God knows every season in life that we go through? They are called seasons because they are temporary, and in these times, God wants you to draw near to Him. If the season you are in now is not so good, then it is nice to know that nothing lasts forever. If you are in a great season, be thankful that you're in it. Regardless of the season, change will continue. What's important to remember is that God is constant throughout them all. He always allows choice, but He wants your utter dependence to be on Him. He wants to be the One that you wake up to, spend the day with, and at night, lay your head to rest with. The closer you draw to Him, the more you will feel confident of your decisions and choices in your season of life.

Genesis 1:2 states that God created the heavens and earth, and Psalm 139 says that God has our days numbered and ordered in life. God is omnipresent; He is everywhere at the same time. This is how we know God knows our seasons. In Jeremiah 1:5, God states that He knew us before we were in the womb and that we were set apart. Is this not enough evidence to know God is with us always? He is everywhere all the time in our every waking breath in all seasons of our lives. It is divine and all-powerful to know that He is present. When you accept the Lord as your Savior and begin to proclaim His declarations over your life, there is no room for anxiety or the fear of the "what-if" mixed emotions about what to do because God gives us self confidence that we cannot get on our own. His Spirit in us guides and leads us. When we have to make choices, the Holy Spirit will bring conviction to us if we need to change our way. God also brings people in to our life for different seasons. We should not ask why they are here one day and gone the next; instead we should praise God for bringing us people to help us, love us, and correct us.

God knows what we need and when we need it. If we can give Him what He is asking for which is our time and the first of our days, our relationship with Him will increase in abundance, and our season in life will be just that, a season.

Behold! Draw near to Him in all of your seasons and He will bring you comfort, peace and joy.

Week 15

DEVOTION

*So it was, when I heard these words
that I sat down and wept, and mourned
for many days; I was fasting and
praying before the God of heaven.
(Nehemiah 1:4 NKJV)*

B ehold! Desire Him! Through prayer and fasting,
God will make His ways known to you.

Nehemiah wept for his city. Have you ever felt such
a love for something or someone that it continually left
you in tears? Or, maybe you wept because of a certain
situation or condition? Anything close to your heart will
touch you through a sense of mourning when it is taken
away or an end is in sight.

Who was Nehemiah? Nehemiah was a cupbearer to
the Persian king and later went on to be a two-time
governor of Jerusalem. Nehemiah was a natural-born
leader who knew how to get things done. When he first

heard of the destruction of Jerusalem, the city walls, gates, and the misplaced people, what did he do? He mourned for days, fasting and praying to God. This was a man of much faith. In fact, he had so much faith that God's hand was on Nehemiah to rebuild the city walls and to restore the people back to their city. God had placed a burden on Nehemiah's heart. Has God placed any burdens on your heart? Maybe it is something that you just can't get rid of. Nehemiah was obedient to the calling. Even through all the struggles of enemies trying tear the wall down, the people stood together armed with spears on the wall while building. Families came together to see their city restored. Nehemiah first prayed to God and asked God for forgiveness of the children of Israel and himself. He also asked God to return back to them. He prayed fervently, and all through the book, he constantly reverts back to asking God to remember him and strengthen him. He was also continually asking the Father to remember His people. Nehemiah fully repented to God for what has happened to Jerusalem. His authentic, unwavering prayers were rewarded by God in heaven. He never stopped striving to restore Jerusalem until the mission was complete.

We can learn so much from the book of Nehemiah. God's ways are a mystery. He appointed Nehemiah for the task because he was in the right place at the right time. Nehemiah was also faithful in his prayer and fasting life. God's glory was shone through Nehemiah. God wants His glory to shine through you. Through prayer and fasting, a two-way conversation is obtained with our Lord. Prayer is a direct communication with God and fasting allows you to be quiet long enough to hear what God wants to say back. Challenge yourself into a day of prayer and fasting and see what God reveals to you.

Behold! He is doing great things through you! Don't stop praying and fasting for guidance.

Week 16

HEART CONDITIONS

And give my son Solomon a loyal heart to keep Your Commandments, and Your Testimonies, and Your Statutes, to do all these things, and to build the temple for which I have made provision. (1 Chronicles 29:19 NKJV)

B ehold! God's love for us is steadfast!
King David prepared a way for the building of the temple. God supernaturally imparted to David the blueprints and exact design of what the temple would look like. God told David that because he was a man of war and had shed blood, his son Solomon would finish the job and succeed David as the king (1 Chronicles 28:3). First Chronicles 29:19, is a prayer from King David to the Lord for his son Solomon.

A loyal heart is a steadfast, constant heart that never fails. Solomon had a great task ahead of him. Can you imagine the weight that was on Solomon's shoulders at different times throughout his reign? Sometimes it is hard to be constant and never wavering when it comes to our faith in the Lord. Solomon did not follow his father's advice toward the end of his life. He allowed his wives to turn his heart from God to other gods. His heart was not faithful.

Each day we make many decisions. Many times we don't even know that the choices we make are all part of our journey that lead us into different things. Our choices have a great impact on our life and our walk with God. That is why it is so important to start the day by worshipping the Lord through prayer and reading His Word. The closer we get to the Lord, our spiritual maturity will begin to bloom. When we ask the Lord to guide our thoughts and decisions for the day, we are leaning on God through faith that He will make our path straight. We are not perfect, but to know and understand what a loyal heart is, will bring us closer to God.

He will reveal His heart for us through His Word and His Spirit in you. He is a good Father who knows us well. We are blessed to know that our Lord is gracious and gives mercy when at times our heart may not be steadfast. It is easy to focus on the problem instead of looking to God for the solution and striving to return to Him with unwavering faith. Ask God today to show you the condition of your heart and to help you make any changes to bring you closer to Him. He has chosen you because you are unique and possess the qualities of sons and daughters of the Most High.

Behold! Press on and stand steadfast! Keep your heart in check through prayer and scripture.

Week 17

HUNGER

For the eyes of the Lord run to and fro throughout the whole earth, to show himself strong on behalf of those whose heart is loyal to Him. (2 Chronicles 16:9 NKJV)

Behold! God is looking for people to show His strength through. He is looking for you.

How hungry are you for God? When you search out the Lord with your whole being, the Lord will reward you greatly. God wants to work through you and your gifting. He is the great Healer, and He wants to use you to show others how good He is. Nothing can be accomplished on our own. We need the Lord day in and out. When we allow the Lord to use us the way that He wants, you will begin to go through a complete transformation of living through the Spirit. New giftings that you never knew about will start to come out as your heart goes through a purification of surrendering to Him. When you die to self and give all of what you have to Him, His power and glory will radiate through you. You will begin to proclaim the power of God over your life and the life of others.

You may be a healer, have the gift of tongues, knowledge, wisdom, teaching, prophecy or discernment. Maybe you have the spiritual gift of impartation imparted in you to give and show others their gifts and to strengthen them in the Lord. There is no limit to what God can do. May God receive all the glory. When you ask the Holy Spirit to fall on you, be ready to see what God can do. God can touch you through prayer or through others. It does not matter how far or close you think you are to Jesus because He is always right here with you. Ask the Holy Spirit to come and open your eyes and to receive what He has for you. Ask God to give you a double portion.

Do you want to be used by the Father? Pray earnestly to Him and tell Him you want to receive supernatural gifting from Him to show others who He is. The light from God will radiate from you when you move from all the "what ifs" to knowing God is greater than all. He knows what we need to be the gift to others. He has us covered. He did not create sickness because He is the great Healer. Ask the Father for an increase. When God gives you your gifting, do not quench it. Our gifts are not limited. God can do anything in and through you. Be open to it. God is glorified through signs, wonders, and miracles, and He earnestly desires to use you.

HUNGER

Behold! Your hunger for God will bring great rewards in your life. God wants to do something through you. God is with you always and wants to use you. You are sons and daughters of the great I am!

Week 18

PAUSE

Be still, and know that I am God; I will be exalted among the nations, I will be exalted in the earth! (Psalm 46:10 NKJV)

B ehold! Pause in the stillness and meditate on who God is.

Selah is a word used in the Bible seventy-one times. It means to pause and to think about (something). Do you incorporate Selah moments in your day-to-day activities? It is so hard to find Selah moments in our busy lives, although we desperately yearn for these moments. We get so overwhelmed from what life throws at us every day that we forget to pause and reflect on what is the most important. Pausing helps us to calmly think and recall what is and is not as important as we think. Maybe your time during the day to take a Selah moment is when you first wake up with a strong cup of coffee or tea. Or maybe when you are driving in the car alone or at night before bed.

Each day, we justify being busy by not wanting to fall behind. Whether it is cleaning the house, shopping for groceries, work, money, bills, appointments, children, meetings, and the list goes on and on and on. Where do we find our Selah moment in the chaos? How can we know who God is if we don't take time to be still? What we don't realize is that each day in itself is filled with things to do and that list follows into the next day. It seems as if we get so wrapped up into the day that we are making idols of all the things we do that we think are so important. Timothy Keller in his book, *Counterfeit Gods*, says that an idol is anything more important to you than God, anything that absorbs your heart and imagination than God, and anything you seek to give you that which only God can give.

We need to learn to incorporate Selah time into our lives to show us that God is control of our every breath we take each day. Selah encourages us to pause in the moment. When we are overwhelmed in daily life, reflect on Psalm 46:10 and remember who you are and where you came from. Silence is sometimes man's greatest friend to hear the voice of God. God is the great comforter who brings strength, courage, comfort, faith, hope, love, and more. Tell yourself today you are ready to fully surrender to the Father who has more for you. It's in the stillness that you will see that God has a greater purpose for us. Don't allow your eyes to be shielded or allow each day to get away from you in busyness. Pray for your eyes to be unveiled in your Selah moments. The enemy loves it when we are doing great things; anything for us to forget what God has for us and anything to not quiet our minds. Be still and know He is God.

Behold! It's in the stillness that God creates his masterpieces in us. Pause and reflect on today's devotional and ask God to give you a heart for more Selah moments.

Week 19

NEW BEGINNINGS

But Ruth said: "Entreat me not to leave you, or to turn back from following after you; For wherever you go, I will go; And wherever you lodge I will lodge; Your people shall be my people, And your God, my God." (Ruth 1:16 NKJV)

Behold! God loves you. Don't lose hope! God will tear down walls to come after you.

Ruth was a loyal, strong, dedicated woman. Ruth, who was Moabite, was also in the line of David and Jesus Christ the Messiah. She bore a child with Boaz, a wealthy farmer in Bethlehem, who was the son of Rahab. Naomi was a Hebrew, and Ruth was a Moabite. There was a famine-causing drought in the land of Bethlehem, and Naomi's husband moved the family to Moab to survive. Do you think Naomi's husband first asked God what he should do, or do you think he made a decision that ended up costing him his life?

Before making any decisions, do you encounter the Lord through prayer? This move was not so good because Moab was oppressed by Israel because of bad decisions. They worshipped many gods. Ruth, being a Moabite, was considered a foreigner, not under the Mosaic covenant. Many practiced idolatry in Moab. Naomi's family settled in Moab, and her sons married Moabite women. This was forbidden under the Mosaic law. Naomi's husband and both sons ended up dying, leaving Naomi a widow with two daughters-in-law. Naomi told them to return to their mothers' houses. She had nowhere else to go but to head back Bethlehem. Both of these ladies had grown to love Naomi; however; in the end it was Ruth who could not be separated from Naomi. Ruth was willing to give up her life, her culture, and everything she believed in to follow Naomi whom she had grown to love and respect.

God desires us, and He wants us to follow Him. Ruth had a special bond with Naomi. Ruth's story is a story of new beginnings. Ruth was a child of God, and you are, too. God was working in Ruth's life from the moment Naomi and her family moved to Moab. God redeemed Naomi who became bitter after her husband and boys died. Ruth married Boaz, a distant relative to Naomi, and he was able to protect and provide for the women. Ruth had a son with Boaz named Obed who was the father of Jessie. Jessie was the father of David (King David) who is in the line of Jesus Christ the Messiah.

The book of Ruth is a story of faithfulness, loyalty, and love. Nothing can stop the power and love of God. God loves all of us, no matter our race, culture, or color. We are all important in God's eyes. Even though Naomi was bitter toward God for the deaths of her husband and sons, God still loved Naomi.

Behold! Restoration and redemption can only come through the Father! He loves you!

Week 20

RESTORATION

Come and let us return to the Lord;
For He has torn, but He will heal us;
He has stricken, but He will bind us up.
(Hosea 6:1 NKJV)

Behold! Come to the Father. He knows our every step we take. He is a good Father!

This is a story of the heart of the Father. Hosea is a metaphoric book showing the reconciliation of a wife and husband and about the restoration of the union of God and Israel.

In hard times, do you stand strong and remain faithful? The story of Hosea is about many things gone wrong. Israel, the Northern Kingdom, turned their back on God. The kingdom betrayed God with much sin. God had chosen them as His people. God chooses us, too. When we choose to change our lives and to follow after our Father, we become changed, dying to self in baptism and being transformed into His image. Just as God chose to save the Israelites by getting them out of exile, when we choose to follow Him, He saves us from ourselves.

The book of Hosea is about God's feelings for Israel. The metaphor in the book portrays a husband whose wife is unfaithful and God telling him to take his wife back. Just as Hosea was distressed and sad over what his wife Gomer was doing, Israel's unfaithfulness has also hurt the Lord, leaving Him upset. Do you feel broken or far from God? He wants to restore you. Call out to Him. The book of Hosea is a love story, the love that God had for the Israelites is portrayed in Hosea and his wife Gomer.

In this world today, sometimes it is hard to remain true to ourselves and to God. God is with us and desires us to return to Him through repenting of our sins and leaving them at the cross. He wants to restore our union with Him. He is the one and only true King who can give us grace and mercy in this life. We are not perfect, and we are living in a fallen world, but God is steadfast and remains the same each and every day. He is never changing and knows that we always need Him—especially when we are struggling and having a hard time remaining steady. Sometimes we trip over our own two feet. He is always there to catch us. When we are in times of despair, He is with us, desiring to draw us near.

Pray to the Father and ask Him to restore you and make your ways known to you. Ask for a revival of self.

Lay down the old ways at the cross and look to what God wants to do today in and through you. Your story is for His glory.

Behold! God loves every piece of you. He has set you apart and has a purpose for your life. Call out to Him. Extend your hands to Him in prayer. Believe.

Week 21

OMNIPRESENT

But Jonah arose to flee to Tarshish from the presence of the Lord. (Jonah 1:3 NKJV)

Behold! He is in the waiting with you.

Have you ever tried to run away from God? What were you fearful of? How did you make your way back to the Father? Were you scared? God is a loving and patient Father. He knew that Jonah did not want to face the people of Nineveh because they were his enemies. God wanted to use Jonah to warn the people to stop acting evil. Jonah was fearful and possibly even scared for his life. God commissioned Jonah to do this assignment for Him, and Jonah was disobedient.

Do you think God broke His relationship off with Jonah because his choice was wrong? God gave Jonah grace. But first, God sent a storm with strong waves and winds when he fled in a boat heading to a different city.

Jonah knew that the storm was caused because he disobeyed the hand of God on His life. He left his calling. He was thrown out of the boat and swallowed alive by a large fish waiting for Jonah as he sunk in the water. Not until Jonah was in the worst place that he could be, did he call out to God in prayer and told Him he was sorry. Have you ever been a Jonah? That is a silly question because we all have been Jonah's throughout life. We also tend not to pray and repent to the Father when things are going well. It is in our worst times that we cry out to the Lord. When we can't take it any longer and have lost all direction in life, we look up to the Lord.

God just does not want us in our dark days; He wants us every day, good and bad. He wants us to pray fervently in good and bad times, when we have lost direction, and when we know exactly where we are going. We carry His Spirit within us, and no matter how far we run, God is still with us. We may think we can run from God, but we can't because He is everywhere. He knows all of our thoughts, good and bad. After spending three days and three nights in the fish, Jonah was finally spit out and knew he needed to turn back to Nineveh and finish the job God gave him. God's mercy endures forever. God's hand was on Jonah, just like His hand is on you.

You are unique in all your ways. Are you running from God? Turn back to the Father. He wants to comfort you. He wants to surround you with His presence. He is waiting for you. God wants to restore you, so come to Him in prayer. He loves you. His arms are open wide waiting for you. He is the everlasting Almighty Father. Without God in our lives, we will falter and break. He is the Great Redeemer. Running will get you nowhere unless you have God with you to fight your battles. He is for you always!

Behold! His promises remain true! He is in the waiting with you. Come Holy Spirit!

AFFLICTION

I am not able to bear all these people alone, because the burden is too heavy for me. (Numbers 11:14 NKJV)

Behold! You are never alone. Your strength comes from the Father!

God gives us strength for today. The hard part is remaining hopeful and faithful when we are in the storm or the struggle. Moses did not think he could do what he was commissioned to do. He did not realize that it was God who was giving Him his strength. When you are tired, weak, and weary, your Father in heaven is calling out to you to lean on Him. Let Him carry you. Put the troubles of today in His hands and watch them close. Give it all to the Father. He knows what is burdening us before we open our mouths. See the goodness in the storm.

When we are tasked to do something that we think is greater than we can ever do, take the reins and step in full force, knowing who your Father is and that He is with you through it all. How do you think Moses felt? Do you think Moses ever felt discouraged? In Exodus 3:11 after God told Moses that he would bring His people out of Egypt, he questioned God by saying, "Who am I that I should bring the Israelites out of Egypt?" God then told Moses that He would be with Him. How powerful is it to know that God is with us! Many times during Moses's assignments, He did not feel qualified for the task. God continually told him that He would be with Him. God said this time and time again to many in the Bible. He is our Father, and we are His children. He will never leave us behind. It is easy to say you know God is with you, and it is another thing to actually put God's words into action and claim them as declarations over your life.

Every season in life and every task we are assigned to are to make us stronger in our identity in Him. Every time we think we can't do it, we should remind ourselves that our Father's Son died for us a painful excruciating death for us to live. Our assignment here on earth is to continue on doing what Jesus Christ the Messiah was doing. Everything that happens in our life is for a reason. We need to spend more time thinking about the good in the junk. We need to find the Jesus, joy, and junk in each day we are given. In what situation did you see Jesus today? Where did your joy come from today? What was your junk like that you had to carry today?

Spending time each day with the Father will increase your strength in Him. You hold the Spirit and power of God within. Be bold; use it.

Behold! God wants you to depend on Him for everything. He gives you strength to get through today. Lean on Him. The task is never too hard when you have God on your side. Your worst day can be beautiful. Pray to the Father for spiritual insight in all you do. Be bold for He is with you!

Week 23

INTERCESSORY PRAYER

*Then the word of the Lord hosts came to
me, saying, (Zechariah 7:4 NKJV)*

B ehold! When you pray on behalf of another, be
ready to see how God is moving.

Are you a prayer warrior? Intercessory prayer is
the most powerful way to pray. When you pray for
another, you are activating transformation and change.
Intercessory prayer definition in the Merriam-Webster
Dictionary is the act of praying in favor of another.
When we pray, we are humbling ourselves and relying
solely on the power of God to move. God wants us to
pray without ceasing. He wants all of our attention.

When we pray for others, we are stepping in the
middle between the Father and the one being prayed
for to release the power of the Holy Spirit to bring an
answer. We are taking on the other's burdens and praying
as if the problem were our own. We are stepping into

the other person's shoes. When you pray for others, do you pray as if the situation were your own? Sometimes we don't even know that another is hurting because we don't take the time to listen. We always want to be heard in this fast-paced world, and we all have our own opinions. If we don't take the time to really listen, we are missing out on what love is. And through listening, the Holy Spirit will activate in you what you need to be praying for them. The Holy Spirit is active in our lives each day. He is waiting for us to see Him and how He works in and through each one of us.

Intercessory prayer is one way of seeing how the Spirit moves in your life and the lives of the ones you are praying for. God is asking you to use this gift and stand in the space for others in need. Intercessory prayer conveys the power of God. Our words become things, and when we release them into the atmosphere, we want our words to breathe life and love. We want to be bold and declare the power of the Holy Spirit. We have all power and authority in us to intervene in other's lives, boldly declare who God is and testify of His miracles. The Holy Spirit has given you the gift of intercessory prayer to rely on God. The more you pray, the more your words will flow, and the Holy Spirit will take over as you will begin to pray from your spirit. We are blessed to have these gifts to enrich our lives. Our Father has given us so many things, and now is the time to take this gift of intercessory prayer and boldly declare what God is doing. Use the power of your words to bring forth trans-formation and change in others' lives.

Behold! You have the gift of intercessory prayer to do the work of His son Jesus Christ the Messiah, here on earth. Use your gift in the name of Jesus. Change and transform lives, starting today. It begins with you and who you are in God. Pray for the perfect will of God for others.

Week 24

EMBRACE

The Lord will guide you continually, And satisfy your soul in drought, And strengthen your bones; You shall be like a watered garden, And like a spring of water, whose waters do not fail. (Isaiah 58:11 NKJV)

B ehold! God is never failing. He will always direct you. Draw close to Him and His spoken words for you. Live close to the Father, and His love will radiate through you. His presence is with you.

No matter where you are in life or what season you are in, this passage is one to hold on to. This verse tells of who our Father is. He is continuously in all we do. He will never leave or forsake you. He will satisfy your soul. This does not mean that He will give you all of your wants; this means that He will supply all of your needs. Come to the Father. Lay down your burdens. He will strengthen you. He will recharge you when you cannot go further.

Do you feel like you are in the wilderness? Lean into the Father. Pray for His guidance and for the Holy Spirit to lead the way. In these times, you may not be able to even think you have an ounce of anything left to give, but just a mustard seed of faith is all it takes. God is powerful and intense, and He will fight for you until the end. When you recognize and believe this, transformation starts occurring. The covering over your eyes will dissipate. You will begin to use His strength in the midst of the struggle, and He will lift and carry you to safe ground.

He is the great Shepherd, leaving no sheep behind. Embrace the struggle with your Father. He is the water you need to survive. His strength is your strength. He is here now. What are you waiting for? Come to the water. Healing begins at His feet. You can never be dry when you're in the arms of the Father. Begin to see yourself as spiritual, one with the Father. Even though you live in an earthly world, you come from God, and He is spiritual. You are more like Him in many ways that you do not see. When you can live in this earthly world but see with spiritual eyes, you will be fully strengthened in Him.

In any situation that life throws at you, recall Isaiah 58:11 and stand firm on what your Father is telling you. He is here and will never leave you. Lift your eyes to Him. He is where all your help comes from. Persevere in the storm. Even when you are tired and weary, call out to the Father. The power of prayer is mighty. He knows what you need before you speak it. He wants you to surrender to Him in good and bad times. He does not want you to lack anything.

Behold! Rely on the promises of God. Write them in your hearts. Study the word of the Lord.

Week 25

INHERITANCE

The Spirit of God has made me, and
the breath of the Almighty gives me life.
(Job 33:4 NKJV)

Behold! God cares about us. He knows us from the inside out. We are made perfect in Him. The Holy Spirit runs the show!

Who do you turn to when you lose confidence? Who do you give credit to in your joy? Job 33:4 is a reminder of where we come from and who we are in the Lord. He always makes a way for us, even when we cannot see it. It is through His Spirit that rests in us, which gives us the confidence to move forward and the joy to be thankful for each day that our Father in heaven has given us. Pray to your Father and ask Him to make a way for you today. Ask Him to open your eyes to see where the Holy Spirit is guiding you. When you read the scripture and see who you are in Him, you can take captive any thoughts that do not come from God. You can declare the scripture in the Bible as you begin each day. By memorizing or writing down scripture, you will be able to reflect on who God says you are in Him. Whether the day is tough or joyful, you will be able to go back to the Word of God and praise Him through prayer.

God gave us the Holy Spirit within us. He loves us so much that He wants us to do His work while we are here. The enemy wants to destroy any work of God, and he will do whatever he can to make us physically or mentally forget who we are in God. God is our only true, firm foundation. That is why prayer and time in the Bible will keep us strong and confident in Him. The Holy Spirit guides and protects us. He gives us giftings. We are steered into moving where the Spirit leads when we tune in and listen.

It is amazing when we can let go of control and let the Holy Spirit take over our lives. It is then that we will begin to see a new transformation in our lives. Our eyes will open to see the new things that our Father is doing. Everything the broken one has been searching for and everything the rich and healthy one has been chasing after will be clear. You will see that the Holy Spirit has been there the whole time with you. God is patient with us. He knows and calls us by name. The choice is ours to make. We can run and chase the world's treasures, or we can run after God and have a heart like His, made in His image, receiving His Spirit, and never being the same again.

INHERITANCE

Behold! He knows us by name! Call out and claim your inheritance of who you are in Him.

Week 26

FASTING

Daniel 10:3 I ate no pleasant food, no meat or wine came into my mouth, nor did I anoint myself at all, till three whole weeks were fulfilled. (Daniel 10:3 NKJV)

Behold! Walking close to God may mean self-denial at times to feel His presence and get a refreshed look into what God wants for you.

Have you ever fasted? Fasting is when you give up food or something else for a period of time to focus on God and to bring you into a deeper fellowship with Him. Fasting is found throughout the whole Bible. People fast for different reasons. Are you in a season of needing guidance on a situation or direction where to turn? Are you fasting out of grief, or are you trying to grow closer to the Lord? Whatever it may be, the power of fasting will help you hear from God. The Spirit within you will awaken and begin to produce next steps for you. Your faith in God will be strengthened, and your relationship with your Father will be stronger. Many promises and blessings come to those who fast with a humble heart. Fasting is a private way to glorify God and gain wisdom. As you gain a closer intimacy through fasting with God, greater spiritual insight will be revealed within you. God is preparing you patiently to receive from Him.

There have been many stories throughout the centuries of those who have fasted and have had great breakthrough. One story in particular is what fasting did for Daniel. Daniel was a man of prayer and fasting. He was preparing and depriving himself to focus solely on God and expecting Him to move in his life. Fasting produces results. The results may look different from what is expected, but you will begin to see the bigger picture. Fasting is a discipline that will bring spiritual growth within you. The next time you need a direct answer, try fasting for twenty-four hours, along with prayer, and journal what God has showed you. During your fast, you may experience many negative things, such as interferences and interruptions. Plan for these things in advance so that nothing can stop you from completing the task.

Can you imagine if everyone fasted? Our society would look completely different. We would be changing the world for the kingdom of God. Lives would be changed, and God's glory would shine through everyone's life. You are sons and daughters of God. Proclaim and declare to others what He is doing! He is doing something new!

Behold! Challenge yourself to a twenty-four-hour fast and feel the presence of God moving in you!

Week 27

PRAYER AND SCRIPTURE

And the Angel of the Lord appeared to him, and said to him, "The Lord is with you, you mighty man of valor!" (Judges 6:12 NKJV)

Behold! The Lord is with you! Don't underestimate the power of God.

What do you do when it comes to making choices? Gideon had an encounter with the Lord, and it is recorded in Judges 6. Gideon saw the Angel of the Lord face to face, and God told him what to do through the angel. The Lord spoke to Gideon and declared to him that he will not die when he faces the Midianites. Gideon had fear, but he continued and did what the Lord said. He was obedient, and God used Gideon to save Israel from slavery. We all have fear at times, but it is what you do with it that changes everything. God is straightforward. The Bible is where God has placed all of His instructions for life. It is up to us to dig into it to find the will of God for our lives. When we need to consider making choices each day in our lives, God wants your choices based on your relationship and faithfulness to Him to be considered first.

Take some time this week to read Judges 6 and notice the similarities in your own life today. Take a mental note on the correlation between the physical and spiritual. Israel had been delivered out of slavery and continued to do evil in the Lord's sight. The children of Israel were once again conquered by the enemy.

Sometimes it takes us many times to learn lessons. God has clearly spoken through scripture what we need to do and how we need to do it, but we tend to put God on the back burner just as the children of Israel were doing. We end up wanting to do what we want each day and do not reflect on what God's will is for us. It is easy to selfishly make decisions now and not think about how it affects our futures. God will begin to teach you and show you how to live by His Word each day, by setting a specific time to read the Bible. The story of Gideon confirms that God is with us always, even when it does not feel like it. He is with us through every choice we make. We can make our choices much easier by turning to the Word of God and praying fervently. Everything we do in our waking lives comes from the Lord.

Behold! Come closer this week to the Lord through His Word and prayer. When making choices look to the Lord first.

Week 28

SURRENDERING

But now, Oh Lord, You are our Father,
We are the clay, and You our Potter;
and all we are the work of Your hand.
(Isaiah 64:8 NKJV)

Behold! As clay is molded into vessels, your Father in heaven wants to mold your whole being into a great work for His purpose to glorify Him and to be used for the kingdom of heaven!

What does it mean to fully surrender to the Lord? As we journey through this life, it is up to God to mold, guide, and walk with us. It is up to us to realize we need Him to make it through this life. God wants us to surrender our lives to Him. He makes it so easy to come to Him. How can we do this in our lives each day? Where can we start? Surrendering to the Lord leads to overcoming in His strength. When you fall, He picks you up. When you are weak, His strength carries you. When you fail, He rebuilds you. Do you need to be restored? Do you trust God enough to surrender all you have to receive His blessings in your life? Life will always bring challenges, and through the trials and temptations, we can look to the Father for restoration. God wants to prepare you through fully surrendering to Him. He wants to use you to bring forth many others to receive and fully submit to Him. You were created for a purpose.

Isaiah 64:8 states that we are the clay. Clay comes from the ground and is formed over time with water, soil, and minerals. The key word is *formed*. When we choose to surrender to the Father, He molds and forms us into His image throughout life. Surrendering makes it so much easier, but sometimes it is the hardest thing for us to do. Once we do it, we wonder why it took so long. Freedom comes through surrendering to the Father. God is the Master Potter over all. He is preparing us to be used by Him throughout life. He is giving us the skills or giftings necessary to do His work here on earth. Come to the Father and surrender your whole being to Him. There is a great awakening that will occur in your spirit when you submit yourself to your Father in heaven. God has a divine plan, uniquely set for you. Try to use a different lens and view what surrendering may look like to you this week. Your spirit yearns to surrender to the Lord.

Behold! He is the Potter, and we are the clay. Surrender to Him, and let Him mold you into the vessel you were created for. You were created to experience heaven on earth!

Week 29

HOLY SPIRIT FILLED

And I have filled him with the Spirit of God, in wisdom, in understanding, in knowledge, and in all manner of work-manship. (Exodus 31:3 NKJV)

Behold! God gives us what we need when we need it. What is it like to be a vessel for God to move in? God filled Bezalel with the Spirit to plan and build the tabernacle. The Spirit also gave the workers skills to accomplish the task. We only see and hear in part because if we knew everything at our waking moment in life, it would be too much for us. God is omnipotent and omnipresent in our lives, and He knows what is needed to get the job done. He uses His Spirit to fill and stir you to get assignments in life done. Our Father cares about us and wants to use us to reflect Him in this life. When we become vessels of God, His light shines through us making us reflect His image in all we do each day. Have you ever had a persistent urge to do something? Or have you ever felt a strong conviction about something? Both of these are the Spirit stirring within you. God is moving in your life and making your way. He wants us to step out of our comfort zone and take steps of faith each day. He wants us to acknowledge when something is not right, so we can make it right.

In Exodus 33:20, God told Moses that no one can see Him and live. In order for God to reach people, He uses His Spirit. That same Spirit is within you when you become a believer in Christ. You choose to leave your old life behind by confessing your sins, asking Christ to come and live in you and getting baptized. When you choose Him, you die to your old life and become a new creation in the Father. Jesus changed everything. He gave us the opportunity to have the Holy Spirit in and on us every day.

The Spirit moved differently in the Old Testament. God placed His Spirit on specific people, but now through Christ, the Holy Spirit is in all believers. We have been chosen, placed here for the purpose of glorifying our Father in Heaven. God wants us to help Him gather His harvest, His people. Just as a child may stray away from their father here on earth, God, our heavenly Father, knows that His children may also stray at times but will return to Him. We are His sons and daughters, and when we recognize who we are in Him, it is a game changer. We no longer have to be held in bondage or living from the past. Our Father makes the way for us each day. Give your first to God and watch Him move in your life!

Behold! Come, Holy Spirit; have your way with us.

Week 30

COURAGE IN THE BATTLE

Have I not commanded you? Be strong and of good courage; do not be afraid, nor be dismayed, for the Lord your God is with you wherever you go. (Joshua 1:9 NKJV)

B ehold! He is surrounding you each day. Feel God's presence in and around you, and lift Him up!

How do you fight your battles? It may seem at times as if you're alone in the midst of strife, but the Spirit of God is always surrounding you. He goes before you to fight your battles. When Moses died, the Lord spoke to Joshua to complete the assignment of getting His children of Israel to the Promised Land. What a huge task that was set before Joshua! Can you imagine how he felt? God told Joshua just as He was with Moses, He would be with him (Joshua 3:7 NKJV). Just knowing that God is with us every day should put a different kind of confidence in us. This passage of scripture today is a great reminder of who God is. This is a great prompting for us each day when we are fighting battles. He is with us, and through Him, we get our strength and courage to continue the fight.

In Joshua, chapter 1, God says time and time again to be strong and courageous. Declare in your life today and this week that God is with you always. He is going through the same motions of the day that you are, and He wants you to lean in on Him. Take this scripture when you are in battle, and remind yourself that wherever you go, your Father is with you. He lights your path each day. He leads the way for you. Listen in the stillness for His sweet voice. Pray to Him. Carry this verse with you, and when you feel weak, pull it out and declare who God is in the name of Jesus! Make your declarations known to the world. Speak them to the atmosphere and stand strong! You are a child of God, and you are ready for each day because He is by your side. You are courageous and strong, and you will continue to move forward because God has confirmed all throughout the Bible that He is with us.

This week, take a moment and reflect on all that has happened and where God showed up. Make a point to reach out to someone in distress and share with them what God is doing in your life. Lift them up and show them how God is in their life also and is helping them also fight their battles. Give them scripture to carry each day and pray with them. Declare who our Father in heaven is out loud!

Behold! Be courageous, bold, and brave as you walk each day, knowing the Lord is with you. Reach out to someone in need and show them who their Father is and what He is doing today.

Week 31

SUPERNATURAL WORKS

I spread out my hands to You; My soul longs for You like a thirsty land. (Psalm 143:6 NKJV)

Behold! He is a good Father. Stretch your hands out to Him; He is where your help comes from.

What is your desire when it comes to God? Who do you live for each day? Give your Father in heaven praise today. Honor Him and adore Him. Pray for God to have His way in you. Have you ever gave all of your heart to something? We all have, and what we learn in life is that everyone in this life will fail us except our Father in heaven. He wants all of our hearts. He wants us to wake and start our day with Him.

What does it look like to live for God alone and still live your every waking breath each day on earth? Start your day with an open heart to live for God. Put Him first and go deeper in your relationship with the Father as many in the Bible did. See the Lord move in your life supernaturally. There are no coincidences in life. Everything is for a purpose. The supernatural works on our behalf as a reminder of who God is.

Take time today and the rest of the week to praise and worship the Lord. Tell Him how great He is. Allow your Spirit within, to let go as you worship the Father. Feel Him in the praise. Now is the time to speak loudly to the Father. Thank Him for all of His works in your life. Reach your arms to heaven and sing loudly to Him. No matter what, He is an awesome God. Nothing and no one can take the place of our Father. Speak everything to the Father as you praise and worship Him. Lift your voice boldly today in prayer, and thank Him for all of His works that you see today in and out of your life! Nothing can steal your joy you have for the Lord. He is so great, powerful, and almighty. His presence in your life is flowing out of you like water of a fresh spring. Your soul gleams as you praise His name.

The Lord fills you with all things necessary for the day. Ask the Father to increase your love and gifting. Share what God is doing in your life today with those who step along your path. Pray for others to feel the Father's love the way you do today. You are a child of God. Ask the Father that when others see you each day, they see Him through you. He is a wonderful Father who loves you so much. His love is never ending.

Behold! Praise and worship the Father each day, and be the light for someone else. Help others to feel the power of His love through you. Desire Him first and foremost in your life and expect great things!

Week 32

GOD'S DEPOSITS

For I know the thoughts that I think towards you, says the Lord, thoughts of peace and not of evil, to give you a future and a hope. (Jeremiah 29:11 NKJV)

Behold! Hold onto the promises that God has for you. Dig into the Bible and take authority over His truths for your life!

We are never lost. He is in control. What does God's promises say to us? What is your hope in? There is freedom in the promises that God gives you. Don't forget what God has already done in your life. He says He will meet all your needs. That does not mean wants. Wants are worldly things. Needs are just one of the many things that your Father in heaven gives you, just as your earthly father gives you shelter. Your heavenly Father supplies your life needs.

As we get closer to God, we mature in Him, our eyes begin to open, and the scales are lifted to see more of who He is—the Great I Am. Nothing can take the love away that He has for us. Is God enough for you today? When we are lost, God pursues us. He never gives up on us. He gives us choice because He wants us to come freely to Him. He wants us to yearn to know Him. He waits patiently for us. Can you see His face today? He is our everything. He hears all of our cries and our joys. Come to the Father today and remember His promises for your life.

No matter what this life brings, hold onto the promises of God. Call on Jesus to supply your needs in times of uncertainty. His promises bring hope and faith into your life. Start your day today by thinking about everything your Father has done for you. Take a moment to praise and worship Him. Write His name on your heart as you move forward with your day. Find your joy and peace today upon the resting promises of God. Receive Him in your thoughts, as you read scripture and in your prayers.

As you go through your day, watch and see whom God brings into your life and thank Him for all of His interruptions to keep you focused on Him and His promises for you. He makes your path clear in good and bad times in your life. He strengthens your spirit as the sun gives life to plants. He rests upon you, waiting for you to recognize Him. He wants you to proclaim to everyone on your life journey who He is and what He has done in your life through His promises!

Behold! His promises stand today and always for you!

Week 33

BELIEF

So they rose early in the morning and went out into the Wilderness of Tekoa; and as they went out, Jehoshaphat stood and said, "Hear me, O Judah and you inhabitants of Jerusalem: Believe in the Lord your God, and you shall be established; believe His prophets, and you shall prosper." (2 Chronicles 20:20 NKJV)

B ehold! In times of uncertainty, remember where your faith comes from.

King Jehoshaphat and his men found faith in God's protection for them. Second Chronicles 20:20 is all about faith. In times of fear, where does your faith come from? Are you facing a season of uncertainty? All throughout the Bible, many men and women have faced times of fear and uncertainty. They all feared the "what if" syndrome of stepping out and letting go of what their minds were telling them. At times in our waking lives, we all face hesitancy. All throughout the Bible, when God puts an assignment on someone, He says, "I will be with you." Is it enough to read those words over and over in the Bible, story after story? He is telling us in the scripture that He is always with us through every experience.

When we read His Word, He is speaking directly to us. God has plans for each one of us. He knows what our life journey looks like. He goes with us into the unknown. He makes our paths straight. We grow and mature through Him, the Bible and prayer. Fear can overwhelm us at times, but we must remember that fear is not of God. Anything negative is from the enemy, outside forces in our lives trying to divert our attention from the Great I Am. We must recognize that there is nothing in this life to fear, and we must learn to take captive these feelings and use our authority invested in us from God to banish these feelings. With God on our side, we can overcome anything. That is faith and God is where it comes from. We can use our faith in all life situations. We will experience uncertainty in life. That is why God has placed others in our life to help us in numerous ways.

We are all vessels for our Father, and when we are obedient to move in the Spirit, God makes a way for us. He shows up in so many ways. Think about how God has showed up recently in your life. Praise Him and thank Him for all He does. There is nothing better than the power of prayer and scripture to strengthen your mind in these times. There is nothing greater than when we can recognize that God is in control of our uncertainty and is making decisions when we let go and let Him.

Behold! You are courageous! In times of uncertainty claim your faith in God for restoration.

Week 34

LOWLANDS

Yea, though I walk through the valley of the shadow of death, I will fear no evil; For You are with me; Your rod and your staff, they comfort me. (Psalm 23:4 NKJV)

Behold! When you are in the valley, keep your trust and confidence in the Lord. He is with you.

Are you going through a valley in life? Valleys are not dead ends. In fact they produce something higher. They give you a higher calling in your walk with the Lord. When we are in the valley, oftentimes we experience all of the negative emotions along with fear and a loss of self-confidence. These are just emotions that we go through as human beings. They are expected when we are not in the best of situations.

God's ways are always on the upswing. You can only stay down for so long before you get up. When you are in the valley, there is no place lower that you can go but up. Thank God for your valley days. Praise Him in the pain. Place your confidence in the great I Am, in the struggle. Then you will be an overcomer of the valley. Picture His hand open for you to put your burden in. Imagine yourself giving your burden physically to the Father and watch Him close His hands on it. Then release yourself from what you cannot control. This essentially means: let go and let God. Then you will upgrade in your spiritual walk with God, and you will be able to accept things that are not so good and keep moving. You will begin to achieve a new level of spiritual maturity within. Living here can be peaches and cream but not every day. We will experience dark valley days, but in knowing that, we also need to know that God is with us through it all.

Find your peace and comfort in the One who loves you. Let Him remove your chains. Pray expectantly. Use your authority invested in you from the Father to move forward and grab the chains that are holding you down and break them! You will find restoration in the valleys of your life. When you walk through the darkness, remember you are with the One who loves you and you're not alone. He will refresh and restore you. Change your mind-set today.

Use your valley testimony to encourage another. Lift them up with your story. Bring them out of darkness. Don't avoid the struggle. Whatever it is that you are facing today, move forward and through it with boldness and courage, the kind that only God can give you.

God cares for you and your well-being. He has proven this time and time again throughout the Bible. Read Psalm 23 this week and read it with fresh eyes. Are you allowing God to lead you in the valleys? As you read, think about all the ways that God has been faithful to you. Journal how God has showed up and reflect on your writing when your mountain has turned into a valley.

Behold! God is your protector when you are in the dark valleys of life. Lean on Him.

Week 35

GLORY REVEALED

*"The sun shall no longer be your light
by the day, Nor for brightness shall the
moon give light to you; But the Lord will
be to you an everlasting light, And your
God your glory. (Isaiah 60:19 NJKV)*

B ehold! God's glory is an everlasting gift
given to you.

When you think about God and His glory, how
would you put words to His glory? Glory is defined as
magnificence or great beauty; high renown or honor
(Merriam-Webster Dictionary). This definition still
makes it hard to put words to God's glory. In the Old
Testament, God was a Spirit, and He displayed His presence by showing glory. He did this often by using fire,
thunder, clouds, or lightening. In the New Testament
when Christ was transfigured on a mountain, Jesus
displayed God in perfect human form. God's glory

97

is revealed all throughout the Bible from creation in Genesis to Revelation where a vision of God's throne is seen in chapter 4. Many of these glory moments in the Bible are known as Shekinah glory moments. Shekinah glory is divine. It is when God's presence shows up as a visitation. One example is with the Israelites coming out of Egypt, God's glory was a cloudy pillar during the day and a fiery pillar during the night to guide the way.

Have you ever asked God to reveal to you more of Him? As you read through the Bible and notice all the times that God has showed up, you will begin to see His glory is everywhere. He has come as the Spirit of God and also as the Son of God. His glory is magnificent! He is all-powerful. If God can do all of these mighty things in the Bible, then He can do these things for you. Ask God to show up today in your walk. Watch how your relationship with the Father improves the closer you walk with Him.

Kathryn Kuhlman was a Pentecostal evangelist famous for her supernatural healings. She was a faith healer. People would come from all over to see her, and before they even entered where she was, many would be healed. She would say she never healed anyone, giving God all the glory. God can and will work through anyone, if only you believe. It starts with faith. Just a mustard seed of faith will open many doors in your walk with God. He wants to reveal to you who He is. He wants to use you as a vessel for others. God will give you just what you need when you need it. Rely on the

Father; His glory is in and on you. You are the example of Jesus. Let your glory shine today!

Behold! Ask God this week to reveal more of who He is to you.

Week 36

UNIQUELY MADE

So God created man in His own image;
in the image of God He created him;
male and female He created them.
(Genesis 1:27 NKJV)

Behold! You were uniquely created for the purpose of telling all who the Great I Am is. Shout it from your lungs; praise Him in worship and prayer today! His presence is with you always.

Everything starts from the inside out. In Genesis 1:27, God made us in his image. How wonderful it is to know that we have been made for His glory! We have a purpose in this life. When our confidence is robbed, we can reflect on this verse to know who we are in Him. He loves us so much that He chose to make us in His image. Just to think about being created in the image of God is a game changer. We often don't even think about this.

When you read this verse, it should make you feel special and unique. You were created for a purpose in this life. No one can take away anything that God has breathed in you. To know we are like the Father not only brings us closer to Him in our walk but also gives a presence of confidence and esteem. His love for us is greater than anything. It is great to have knowledge, but to have the love of God in and with you each day surpasses anything this world can offer.

Once we see who we are in the Father, we can move forward into being servants and stewards for Him. We can show love and compassion for others by how we live out each day. We can give this precious gift of Genesis 1:27 to others so that they can experience the same walk you are experiencing with God.

Can you imagine if everyone knew that God created him or her in His image? Can you imagine how this world would look? This world would reflect an Acts 2 church. Lives would change, and the enemy would no longer be effective. Jesus has already won that battle. When we rest on the scripture of who we are in Him, we are prepared for any battle in life.

God has given us His Word; He has said He is with us always, and His Words reflect the armor that we wear each day. His truth sets us free. There is freedom in the name of the Lord. Come get your freedom today through the Father. Stand firm on His Word, and let His strength carry you forward. God wants all of His children to be confident in who they are in Him. Sons and daughters will prosper in good and bad times. Nothing can steal your heart away from God when you are aligned with Him. He loves you!

Behold! This week, be a steward of the Lord by sharing with others who they are in Him.

Week 37

MIRACLES

*He is your praise, and He is your God,
who has done for you these great and
awesome things which your eyes have
seen. (Deuteronomy 10:21 NKJV)*

Behold! Miracles show evidence of God and His almighty power.

Miracles have the power in them to change lives today just as they did throughout the Bible. The Bible is a miracle because power lives in each story. As you read the miracles of yesterday, your eyes will be open to seeing that they have never ceased. Miracles are all around you today. Where have you seen miracles change lives in your daily walk? Miracles throughout the Bible give us confidence to do the work of the Lord. Through the giftings given to us by the Holy Spirit, God moves in and through us to accomplish tasks designed to bring glory to Him. Once we know our gifting, we can begin to bring it to life each day, and you will begin to see miracles taking place in the lives of others.

What God has given us is not meant to be kept in a closet or just for our own use. These special qualities given by God are meant to restore life on earth as it is in heaven. We have been chosen to help God gather His harvest, His people. To do this, we must remain close to the vine, to Him. We must rely on the Holy Spirit to move us each day. We must be willing to take great steps of faith out into the unknown. God has promised to always be with us, and we must never forget His presence. The more we put our trust and faith into the Father, the more He will reveal to you who He is. He will also assign you to more tasks here on earth.

Are you ready to take on the world for God? Are you ready to see miracles happening each day? People in this world today are broken and hurt. Some do not know which way is up. As sons and daughters of God, you are commissioned to carry the gospel with you each day and share who Jesus is. The gospel travels through relationships, and it starts with you. God wants to use you to help others. We have been commissioned to bring men and women out of darkness into the light of the Father. You are a child of God, and He is with you always. He will guide and protect you throughout your life. In your weakest moments, the Father will carry you.

Deepen your faith in Him by reading His Word each day. Take time to pray and to stand in the gap for others as you pray for them. Come to the Father today with an open heart and willingness to take boldly what He has for you. God has His hand on your life. He has your name written on Him. He will always remember you.

Behold! At the end of your life, when God asks you what you have done for Him, what would you like to say?

STANDING IN THE GAP

*So I sought for a man among them who
would make a wall, and stand in the gap
before Me on behalf of the land, that I
should not destroy it; but I found no one.
(Ezekiel 22:30 NKJV)*

B ehold! The power of intercessory prayer brings
mighty rewards! Stand in the gap for someone.

Intercessory prayer is when you pray for someone
else. At times, you may step in and pray for someone
who has either given up or maybe is too weak to pray.
When you do this, you are essentially taking their place
and praying as if the situation is your own. There is
power to intercessory prayer. As sons and daughters of
the Most High, we have authority to step in and act on
what is needed. Prayer changes everything, and that is
why it is so powerful. Have you ever thought of prayer
as a tool of weaponry? When we take up the burden for

another, we are covered by the promises of God. Job 42:10 states that the Lord restored Job's fortunes when he prayed for his friends, and the Lord gave him twice as much as he had before. God knows our heart inside and out. He knows what condition we are in when we come to Him. Intercessory prayer destroys the work of the devil. Are you ready to lay down your life and stand in the gap for the one in need? Ask God what He wants you to specifically pray for before you begin.

As a vessel of God, praying for others is something that comes naturally. When a loved one, a friend, or a stranger is in distress, what do you do? Many times we don't think to pray first. Many times we get caught up in what is happening and try to comfort in other ways. It's wonderful to support others, but knowing that you have a gift that you carry with you always, that has the power to do signs, wonders, and miracles in others' lives is a treasure bestowed in you.

The next time you come upon a situation that requires the hand of God through intercessory prayer, be bold and claim your right to do the work of the Lord. Watch and see how intercessory prayer changes your life and the life of others. Intercessory prayer is living from the kingdom of God. As sons and daughters, it is our obligation to allow the Holy Spirit to work through us. As you pray this week, ask God to bring to your attention anyone who is in need of intercessory prayer. God will guide you in all you do when you come to Him open and ready to receive.

Behold! Jesus stood between God and man, died for us and sits at the right hand of the Father still standing in the gap for us.

Week 39

SONS AND DAUGHTERS

*Now give me wisdom and knowledge,
that I may go out and come in before
this people; for who can judge this
great people of Yours? (2 Chronicles
1:10 NKJV)*

B ehold! Wisdom is established through time. Ask
God today for His wisdom to guide you.

Solomon was in the presence of God at the bronze
altar in front of the tabernacle of God that was prepared
by his father David. In 2 Chronicles 1:7, God appeared
in the evening and asked Solomon what he wanted.
Solomon did not ask for riches, wealth, honor, or the
life of his enemies, but he asked for wisdom and knowledge to judge God's people. God knew Solomon's heart,
so He bestowed on Solomon wisdom and knowledge.
He also gave him riches, wealth, and honor, which was
something no king ever had been granted before or after

him. Solomon wanted to be a good king to the people; that is why he asked for wisdom and knowledge.

When you come to God through prayer or just speaking to Him during the day, what do you often ask God for? As you read 2 Chronicles this week, you will see that even the best intentions or heart can quickly go south. Solomon had everything a man could ask for, but he also had choice. When we allow our mind to take over, at times the decisions we make are not aligning with the heart of God. We get caught up in the moment and our wisdom of who we know God is can go out the door. Instead, we start thinking what we want, and the goodness of what God has given us quickly turns into something not so good.

We are blessed to have a God who loves us so much that through repenting of our wrong choices, He will restore us through forgiveness. He will get us back to where we were. His grace is sufficient for us, and only our Father can give us mercy and grace. His plans for us are so much bigger than the world we live in. He wants us to help Him restore heaven on earth. When we choose Christ to come and live in us through baptism, our relationship with God changes greatly. We begin to see that we are His sons and daughters, and He has purposed our lives to be a light for others.

Solomon achieved great things for God, just as you achieve leaps and bounds in your waking life for the Father. During his spiritual decline, he obtained many flaws, but God showed him that it is not enough to say sorry. All of Solomon's ways needed to turn around and show a godly walk in life. When God blesses you with answering a prayer today, be it wisdom, health, knowledge, or more, remember who you are in Him and ask the Lord each day to make your ways straight and your decisions good. Your help comes from the Father. Let Him guide your choices each day.

Behold! Turn to the Father today and tell Him you are ready to receive what He has to give you.

DIVINE REVELATION

Then the Lord opened the mouth of the donkey, and she said to Balaam, "What have I done to you, that you have struck me these three times?" (Numbers 22:28 NKJV)

B ehold! His presence is with us. We are carriers of His Word and Spirit. Miracles are all around us.

Do you believe in miracles? A miracle is defined as a surprising and welcome event that is not explicable by natural or scientific law and is therefore considered to be the work of a divine agency (Dictionary. com). In Numbers 22:28 Balaam was not receiving the Lord's guidance, so God needed to get his attention by speaking through a donkey. God was trying to open Balaam's eyes. Balaam's mission was not the mission that God had in mind, and He needed to get his attention to change his ways. This story is definitely a divine work of God.

God is all-powerful and can do anything at any time to grasp your attention. Miracles happen for many reasons. God wants us to fully surrender and rely on Him. There is only one judge in this life, and it is our Father in heaven. He is continually shaping and molding us. Sometimes He needs to get our attention, and He will provide a miracle for us to see to help us change our way of thinking. We could receive a miracle from sickness to healing, news that you never thought you would hear of, or miracles may happen around you with other people. Maybe someone is in need of money and it comes right when it is needed.

Whatever it may be, miracles are always all around us. There have been countless stories from hospitals of unexplained miracles of healing when the odds did not look good. There simply was no explanation. We should not focus on the why, but praise and thank our Father in heaven for providing once again. God provided the Israelites many miracles to get them out of Egypt and into the Promised Land. They continued to do things that were not so good in the Lord's eyes.

Are you or someone you know in need of a miracle today? Start today by choosing to live in the supernatural world of our Lord. Stay in the moment and walk forward through the struggle with the promises of God. Love the struggle. God is walking with you each day, no matter how good or bad it may be. Expect miracles.

Focus on what God will do in the unraveling. Unshaken faith in God is for *all* seasons in life. Ask the Father to refocus your lens today to see the many miracles He is doing in your life right now. Ask the Father to show you these miracles so that you can lift someone else up today that is in need.

Behold! Shift your attention on the miracles that God is providing you today in this moment.

Week 41

THE FATHER'S LOVE

The Lord your God in your midst, The Mighty One, will save; He will rejoice over you with gladness, He will quiet you with His love, He will rejoice over you with singing. (Zephaniah 3:17 NKJV)

Behold! God's love surrounds you each and every day. Today pray for Him to have His way with you. God's love surpasses all of our knowledge. We cannot know the depths of His love for us because He is a limitless God, and we are limited. We are not supposed to know the complexity of His love. Our faith in the Father and to feel His love should be enough; knowing who He is should sustain us each day. God reveals His love to us unselfishly. When we choose to read His Word each day and pray, His love radiates throughout our total being. His love is showcased on display when we take His love and give it to someone else.

It is in the stillness where His love is magnificent. He wants us to dedicate alone time for Him each day so that He can show us how much He loves us. He is working in your life right now as you read this devotional. His presence is stronger than any pull. He wants to welcome you into His world, which compliments Him greatly. His beauty arises within you as you start your day by putting the Father first. Come to the Father this morning with high expectations of feeling His presence and carrying it with you throughout your day. His love brings peace to chaos, joy to pain, and comfort to uncertainty.

As you welcome the Father into your everyday life, watch the transformation of your heart unfold. Your eyes will begin to unveil and see this perfect love that can only come from our Maker. He provides the miracles of life each day. He unfolds His Words to you as He is maturing and strengthening your roots. Love is powerful and almighty. It can only come from a personal relationship with your Creator. Love surpasses all knowledge. Love conquers all things.

God wants you to take what He has given you and share it with others you encounter each day. Let God's love glow from your being. You are a shining star for the whole world to see. Let your light shine among others today! The choice is yours to focus on the truth of the Father or go about your day as if nothing is happening in and around you. His glory is so radiant that you will not miss a beat when you choose to love the Father the way He loves you. What He gives you is always for the purpose of His kingdom. You are sons and daughters of the Most High. Recognize who you are today and take bold steps of faith to prosper in the Fathers eyes!

Behold! The love of the Father cannot be bound. Bask yourself today in His presence.

Week 42

REPENTANCE AND RESTORATION

Keep your heart with all diligence,
For out of it spring the issues of life.
(Proverbs 4:23 NKJV)

B ehold! Your feelings are reflected by the state your heart is in. What is the state of your heart?

The heart is mentioned throughout the Bible more than 1000 times. This five-letter word has great significance in our lives. The heart can make or break us. We can live righteous and holy or sinful and disgraceful from our hearts. The choice is and has always been ours. Put yourself to the test today by examining your heart. Journal the good, bad, and the ugly that your heart has experienced. Now ask God to remove anything in your heart that is not of Him. Ask Him to guide you into a reckless love with Him. Journey into the unknown by trusting God to do the work of restoring your heart being fully committed to Him. He will show you mercy and grace. He will begin to flow through you like a tidal wave. You will want to express all the exuberant feelings that the Lord is making in you. Journal the whole process so that you can look back and reflect how God has been working in your life.

The heart is a major scale in life that balances our emotions, helping us to make correct choices each day. Everything you think stems from how you feel in your heart. Sin comes from the heart, just as virtue also does. When you speak, you reflect the state of your heart at that exact time. If you are full of goodness then your life will reflect goodness. What you believe reflects the type of life you choose to live. It starts in the heart. How is your heart today? Everyone has bad days, but it is up to us to let go and let God. The choice is ours to remove anything that does to come from God.

When the heart is not doing well, it will mirror image what it is feeling with life issues that you may be going through. Examine your heart each day, and choose to not allow the enemy to get in and disrupt your day. Give it all to God, and watch what He does with your life. He is a God who restores. He loves you so much that He patiently waits by your side to choose Him to be the ruler of your life.

This world can offer us nothing compared to the great love of God. He is the one who purifies and cleanses us each day. Come to the Father today; lay down your burdens at His feet. Ask Him to remove anything that does not come from Him. Ask all in the name of Jesus. Let the Holy Spirit stir in you and move you into a deeper relationship with the Father. As you move into great depths, allow your Father to cleanse and prepare you for greater things to come. He holds the key to your life. Only God can overcome what you are facing. The Spirit speaks through your heart.

Behold! Examine your heart each day, confess your sins and thoughts, and pray for restoration.

Week 43

THE CHOSEN ONE

And I will put enmity, Between you and
the woman and between your seed and
her Seed; He shall bruise your head,
And you shall bruise His heel. (Genesis
3:15 NKJV)

Behold! Our Savior, Jesus Christ the Messiah was planned all along.

Jesus is found throughout the whole Bible. Do you see Him in both the Old and New Testament? God prepared the way for His son to come and do the unimaginable. He came to restore God's plan for humanity. He was chosen to come to die for us so that we can live and carry on what He was doing here on earth. Genesis 3:15 is describing Jesus who is to come. Jesus is the seed. Going back to the beginning, Jesus was already there in the making. God, being all-knowing, knew that there would be a feud between the enemy and Jesus. The seed is the promise of the One to come. In time, Jesus came and took away all our sins. He gave us a chance to be in complete union with Him by choosing to give up the life we had and begin a new life in Him. God made a way out for us. He issues no more commandments because He now writes them in and on our heart. Conviction plays a key role in knowing when we are about to do something not so good. That conviction is the Holy Spirit within us that pokes at us when things are not right. The Holy Spirit comes to live in us as believers in Christ. We are so blessed to have a Father in heaven, who will fight for us until the end.

So many have let God down in the past. How do you think He felt when he simply told Adam and Eve to refrain from one thing and to reproduce and grow His garden? We were created to populate the earth for the Lord. The task was so simple, and it was messed up just like that. Eve ate from the one tree that God forbid. She also fell into temptation of the serpent rather than fleeing from him. She was disobedient. Her choice changed all of the coming future of humanity.

When God calls you to do something or when you feel a conviction not to do something, how do you respond? Do you run and flee from temptation? Do you step out into faith when your call is specific to what God is asking, knowing that God has your back to reach the goal? Jesus is the promised Seed because He brought deliverance to us all by destroying the evil works of Satan. We are free when we choose to give our lives to

Jesus. The Bible is a testimony of how God loves us. Take time this week to find Jesus all throughout the Bible. You will be amazed in the places you will find Him!

Behold! The cross has the final word. Jesus' death destroyed what Satan wanted to accomplish.

Week 44

BRAVERY

*For if you remain completely silent at
this time, relief and deliverance will
arise for the Jews from another place,
but you and your father's house will
perish. Yet who knows whether you have
come to the kingdom for such a time as
this? (Esther 4:14 NKJV)*

B ehold! Bravery is something that God has instilled
in you from before you were thought of.

Queen Esther is a story of courage and bravery.
Have you ever been in a place where you had to make
a major decision? Esther had a wonderful life living as
a queen, married to the king of Persia. The king had no
idea that she was once an orphan Jew. God had a challenge in store for Esther. God had purposed her life to
save her people. Esther had a huge decision to make.
Was she going to save her people, or was she going to

124

continue to live safe? Have you ever wanted to just continue to sail smoothly in life, not wanting to confront any problems? Mordecai, Esther's cousin, was about to rock her world. Nothing happens in life by coincidence. God has predestined our lives but also has allowed us to make our own choices in the process. He says He knew us before He formed us in the womb. Esther was made to be a woman of courage.

You are made to take bold steps of courage in your life each day. God has shown you time and time again that He is with you. With the faith, hope, and love that you carry within you, you can courageously step out and overcome anything. The Holy Spirit in you empowers you to take charge. All you have to do is trust God with each day that you are given. Don't let intimidation or fear overcome you. Those things are not of God. Recognize what God has given you to fight all your battles.

God has given you the gift of strength and His words in the Bible, which reflect power to you as you read them. Stand firm in courage today in whatever decisions you will make. Know that God is with you. Pray and read His Word to guide you. Listen in the stillness for His voice and journal your thoughts. It is in your thoughts that you will hear God. Give to God any negative emotion you encounter and press forward. Your identity is in God, and knowing this will encourage you to take steps of faith each day. Rest in the Lord's strength that He has for you. Every day that you rely more on Him, your faith increases. Keep your eyes fixed on the

Lord as you move throughout the day. Stay connected to the Vine.

Behold! Today be strong in the Lord and put on His armor. Be rooted in Him; His love is grand.

Week 45

LIVING WATER

*And it shall be that every living thing
that moves, wherever the rivers go, will
live. There will be a very great multi-
tude of fish, because these waters go
there; for they will be healed, and everything will live wherever the river goes.
(Ezekiel 47:9 NJKV)*

Behold! Carry the glory of God with you by spreading the story of Christ.

Christ is the living water that we all need. This Water is here for all of us to take advantage of. Once we choose to have Jesus come live in us, we then are assigned a new way of life. Becoming a believer of Christ puts a great responsibility upon all. God's authority now rests in us. He is the fruit our Spirit yearns for. As Christian believers, we must answer the call of the Lord to spread the Good News. God's son came and died a horrific death for us to live. We owe our lives to the Lord. It's time to lay down our selves and live for our Father in heaven as sons and daughters of the Most High. God has bestowed spiritual blessings upon each one of us. It is up to us to find these gifts and use them for God's glory. Through Him flows the river of life. Through Him healing occurs. As believers, we have these special gifts to be used for others to show them the one true way.

The gospel travels through relationships. Each life that we encounter has the opportunity to be transformed by our words. Have you thought about how you can change someone's life today by sharing what Jesus has done for you? As you move through your week, think about how you can take bold action for the Lord. Think about how you can make the change in your own life and the lives of others. God's fruit for you is in the blessings that He bestows upon you for others. Focus on being a messenger of God, carrying His light in you.

Today is a great day to start by being an example of who God is. Let the river flow out of you and present itself as God sees fit for all who cross your path. When we choose to let Jesus in our hearts, life increases with great growth. Our spiritual maturity in who He is multiplies the closer we stay connected to Him. By releasing the gospel to others, we are creating heaven on earth. We are building the kingdom of God here. Help God gather His harvest of people by using your gifts that the Holy Spirit has given you. There is freedom in living as sons and daughters of the Father. Come to the Father and drink from His water. Take your God-given authority, and use it to make glorious changes in the world today. He is with you always.

Behold! Hold onto Jesus. He must increase, and we must decrease for His glory!

Week 46

THE POWER OF GOD

Then God said, "Let there be light";
and there was light. (Genesis 1:3 NKJV)

Behold! God almighty is all-powerful and everlasting!

Genesis 1:3 tells us that with a single word spoken, life became known. The world was created. There is nothing more powerful than the Word of God. We also have His Spirit in us and can shake the world we live in by resting in His Word. With the faith of a mustard seed, we can transform our life and other lives that surround us. As believers, the power of God is acknowledged in our lives through His strength in us. He makes a way for us. We are tools to be used by Him.

Can you see what God is doing in you? You are clothed in the power of God. His righteousness covers you. Are you looking for a spiritual upgrade in your Christian walk with the Father? Are you in need of a spiritual awakening? Ask the Father to place His hand over your life and the decisions that you make each day. Let God's power be your deciding factor in all situations. Let Him guide you. He holds the key to your life.

Think about what motivates you with your walk with God. Will you let His Spirit in you navigate your life? You can go through any depth with the Father by your side. He makes the waves of life smooth. In the fierce storms of life, He brings calmness. Walk out to Him on the water. Picture Him surrounding you as you move in and out of the days. He releases a power that strengthens your soul. Your heart is conditioned by His voice.

Is control something you struggle with? Give it to the Father. Let go and place any feelings of uncertainty and fear in His hands. Watch these things leave you and enter His hands. Now watch His hands close and remove these burdens from you. His power is all around you and releases your breath into the air. Grasp the power of the Most High in your waking moments. In your dreams, converse with the Father to take you into deeper depths, calming you as you move through the waves. When you awake, you will feel refreshed, knowing you are connected to the Father.

Think about where you might be today in your journey with the Lord. Don't lose grasp. Hold on tight, and let His power consume you. He is a mighty God and can do anything. Don't dismiss what His Word says. Dig deep into the Bible and allow His words to flow in and out of you. Let God be your voice each day. Speak into the lives of those close to you and anyone who you come in contact with. Use the power of God to lift others up. Proclaim what His Word says. Be a conduit of the Lord. Let your journey begin today with the power of God.

Behold! The power of God is uncontainable. Reach out and claim His power over your life!

Week 47

SUBMISSION

You shall rise before the gray headed
and honor the presence of an old man,
and fear your God: I am the Lord.
(Leviticus 19:32 NKJV)

Behold! Consecrate yourself to the Father today and see the many wonders He provides.

God is clearly telling us who He is in this scripture. During this time, it was a Jewish custom to rise out of respect for the elders. We are required to show honor to others just as we are to fear God and honor Him as the most divine of all. When you think of who God is, what are your thoughts? God gives us favor in this life. Each breath we breathe is because of God's good will toward men. When you come to the Father, is it in full submission, full of honor and respect? God is more than what He does in our lives and the lives of others. He is all-powerful. He created the world with a word. That is huge! His son became Man, first being a Word. Think about that for a minute. First, He was a word. Then, He became Man.

We never really think about the deep stuff when we are reading the Bible or praying. Most of the time to be honest, when we pray, we are asking God to fix a problem or us. We are coming to Him selfishly to not have to feel the way we do. Whether it is pain, sickness, mental or physical disease, divorce, or death, that is when we usually are at the bottom of the pit and cry out to the Lord. This is a great time to rest in who He is, but a greater part of the mess would be not to forget that God brings us out of the struggle. Then it is our job to share the unraveling to others and give God the credit.

As you go through the week, think about other ways that you can fully submit to God by coming to Him, our sovereign Father, and praying for others. Ask the Father to grow your maturity in Him. Ask the Holy Spirit within you to guide you into the unknown that requires faith, hope, and trust in the Lord. God knows all of you. He knows your troubles and burdens. He wants to know you more than your brokenness. He wants to use you for the kingdom of heaven. The closer you get to Him and the deeper you fall in love with Him, He will reveal more and more to you. He wants you to fully depend and rely on Him for everything in this life. He wants you to thank Him for things more than material possessions. Come to the Father today and see all of Him and His beauty through the nature around you. Yes! He made the flowers, the sky, the waters, the air that we breathe, and more. Everything has a specific purpose here on earth for us to survive. See the Father in a new light today, and let Him wrap you up in His glorified presence.

Behold! Fully submit yourself to the Father by surrendering your total being to Him today.

NEW WINE

Look among the nations and watch-Be
utterly astounded! For I will work a
work in your days, Which you would
not believe, though it were told to you.
(Habakkuk 1:5 NKJV)

B ehold! Sometimes it is hard to believe that God
will show up and rescue us in the battle. He
comes for us because we are His, and He will never
leave us behind.

Have you ever wondered how God shapes us? Have
you ever considered that it is in our breaking moments
when God reveals who He is and the power He has to
make us new again? God brings us into new horizons
as He shapes us through our deepest darkest moments.
The more we lift Him up in these times, the more of His
glory falls upon us. We begin to experience who God
is in our shattering moments. The Lord is all-knowing,

and He hears us at all times. The Father's voice brings us to life. He creates the luminescence surrounding us. His Spirit breathes out of us. We are transformed into His image through the shaping. When we give all of the glory to God for what He is doing in our lives, the kingdom of heaven and all the angels sing praises to the Lord our God, the almighty Father.

In your struggle, drop to your knees and praise the One who gives grace and mercy. Cry out to the Lord and thank Him for His presence and the unraveling mystery that He is doing within you. It's a bittersweet moment to give all you have to the Father because of the fear of letting go and allowing His presence to take over every inch of your identity. Our identity was never our own to begin with; it is in the Father. Cry out to Him, desperate to hear His voice. He is there. He always shows up. Bask in His presence, and feel Him surrounding you. Feel His glory in you. Experience God in raw form as you pray. Don't stop.

There is no limit to how long you stay in His presence. Stay where you are until He is done with you. This is a beauty-for-ashes moment. Love the struggle as you let go and let God have His way with you. Let all of the emotions flow in and out of you freely. Don't question them; just let them pass through. Can you feel the love of the Father? He loves you so much. He is restoring you as you fall deeper, intertwined to Him. When you come back to the present from worshipping Him, you will feel new and ready to begin again.

Behold! His love for you is greater than anything that is materialized. Nothing can measure it.

Week 49

INSCRIPTIONS

*See, I have inscribed you on the palms
of My hands; Your walls are continually
before Me. (Isaiah 49:16 NKJV)*

Behold! Throughout all of our good and bad seasons of life, God will never forget us.

This scripture is about the return of Israel from being banished. God's love is everlasting. He will not forget His children. Time and time again, the Israelites had sinned, but God never gave up on them, just as God will never give up on you. God created us because He loves us, and He wants us to fulfill His plan laid out in scripture. As believers, we have a responsibility that we owe to God. At the end of our lives, it will not be good enough to say that we worked thirty years from 8 a.m. to 5 p.m., got married, raised children, went to church, and lived well. God wants so much more for us. He wants us to delve into the fire of life.

He wants us to take chances and experience what life offers us. All of this within reason. Our Father in heaven wants us to live for Him and to spread the Good News of Jesus Christ. He wants us to be fruitful and multiply. The earth is His garden. As Christians we are called to more. We are His sons and daughters, and we are called to fight the good fight in life. Take the bull by the horns each day. Be the light for others in your life. Show people who God is by the way you live and how you live life.

Be bold and courageous. Don't back down from what the enemy will throw at you. God has promised us that He will always be with us. Isaiah 49:16 states that He will not forget us because we are inscribed on His hands. He wants to use us as vessels for Him. At the end of our lives, when we approach the almighty One, what will you have to say to Him? What if God asked you what you did in this life for Him? What would you say?

Take time this week to think about these questions. Reflect on your answers by journaling them. As you step outside your house each day, think about how you can be used by God. Ask God to take control of your life and your Spirit. Ask Him to use you for His glory and the kingdom of heaven. You can't go wrong with God on your side. He will never forget you, just as a mother will never forget her children. You are a child of God and He has and wants more for your life. You are safe in the arms of the Father. He restores you and equips you for the battle. Your strength comes from the Father.

His love is everlasting. Share the love of the Father today. The gospel travels through relationships. Get to know someone today. What is holding you back? God wants to show you favor today. Experience the love of the Father through a new friendship. He is in the waiting for you. His loves never changes.

Behold! Step out in bold faith today, knowing the Father has your name inscribed on His hands.

Week 50

EXPECTATIONS

And Enoch walked with God; and he
was not, for God took Him. (Genesis
5:24 NKJV)

Behold! The power of the Holy Spirit lives in you
to give you a flawless trust in God as Enoch had.
Come, Holy Spirit; teach us to faithfully live by the
Word of God and be good stewards.

Can we experience the same act of walking with
God as Enoch did? What does walking with God look
like to you? There is very little to be known about Enoch
in the Bible. We know that he lived for 365 years (Gen.
5:23). We also know that he was one of the oldest living
people in the Bible. Enoch was a prophet, one who held
the vision of God and who preached the Word of God.
Let's focus on the first part of the verse: Enoch walked
with God. He had a close relationship with the Father.
This is something that we are all capable of doing. The

question is: Do we want to invest in more of our time during the day to get to know our Father in heaven? How much of the day do we want to "fill" up avoiding God and filling tasks up to check off our daily lists? We know that tomorrow is full of more lists that we create to stay "busy."

Enoch is a short but sweet story. It is about having trust in the Lord. Along with trust comes faith. Faith is having a strong belief in God—believing in the super-natural and believing in the God that you cannot see in physical form but knowing that He is very real and tangible. Faith is expecting that one day we will be in God's presence in heaven. We will be walking with Him and taking part with Jesus in judging the world as we know it and the angelic beings. This is what we know as Christian believers will become part of our future. God is a mystery, and He reveals to us what we need to know when His timing is right. As sons and daughters of the Lord, we are set apart because we have chosen to surrender our total being to Him.

Enoch fully submitted to God. His life and his works show this to be true. You may be asking yourself where you can fit in time to meet with God. It's easy. Give God the first of your day. When you wake up, commit to spending a certain amount of time in the Bible, praying and listening in the stillness for Him. Or maybe your schedule is sporadic and your first of the day is in the evening or at lunch. Whatever it may be, God is in the waiting for you to search Him out. He wants a deeper relationship with you. Challenge yourself to one week of getting to know God more than you have before. Journal in this time to recall on what occurred during these moments. See how your life unfolds and transforms as the future weeks come. See how you develop a sense of peacefulness in your spirit.

Behold! He is with you and wants more of you. God is a jealous God. Give Him your first.

Week 51

NEW CREATIONS

As in water, face reflects face, So a man's heart reveals the man. (Proverbs 27:19 NKJV)

Behold! Jesus is the key to your heart.

What we are feeling on the inside often reflects through our personality and the way we carry ourselves—how we communicate to others. We can't get through life having a perfect day each day, but we can recognize when we are having an off day and take it to the Father for restoration. Through our relationship with God, our faith continues to grow. Our faith and trust in the Lord helps us to grasp our not-so-good days a little better. God gives us hope in uncertain times.

What does it mean to have a pure heart? Our hearts are hidden beneath skin and bones. God made us alike in this area but unique as individuals. When we choose Christ as our Savior, we get new hearts. Our bodies will still get old as time goes by, but our inner appearance will be new and fresh as a child in the eyes of God. Our thoughts, desires, personality, and identity all come from the heart. A pure heart is transparent, meaning there are not hidden agendas within. The only person who can make a pure heart in us is Jesus Christ. He is the only way to the Father. Making the choice to surrender to Jesus, asking forgiveness for our sins, and being baptized will make us new inside and out. You may not see many outside changes, but from within, you will have a new innocent heart, and your outside will reflect it. Your heart will be new, like an infant.

Jesus died and sacrificed His life for us. God wants all of His children in the kingdom of heaven. Just as the shepherd leaves no sheep behind, God will never leave you behind. If you have not given your life freely to Jesus and you would like to, come to Jesus now. Ask Him to forgive you for your sins. Tell Him you want to commit your life to following Him and surrender your old self to Him. Let Him know that you know He sacrificed His life for you to live a new fresh restored life in Him. Tell Jesus that He is the only way to the Father, and today you want to continue to live your life as a son and or daughter of the Most High.

The Father wants to create in you a new heart today. This is called salvation. Declaring that you want a new life in the Father and to leave your old life behind. He will never forsake you. If you are not attending a church, reach out today to friends and relatives and start trying out some churches that fit you well. The next step is to get baptized, leaving your old self behind and letting God make you a new creation. He will renew your spirit. The past is behind you. Focus on today and what God is doing in you.

Behold! When you give your life to Jesus, your heart will become pure. You are a new creation!

HEAVENLY ASSIGNMENTS

The counsel of the Lord stands forever,
The plans of His heart to all generations
(Psalm 33:11 NJKV)

Behold! Trust in the Lord and obey His ways for you. God's purpose for our life is higher than what we can imagine. God used many people throughout the Bible for the purpose of the kingdom of heaven. The Old Testament promise of God was His people, the children of Israel and the restoration of the nation. The New Testament people of God have a different purpose today: it is Jesus, the promised One to come. It is our calling to follow Jesus once we accept Him into our hearts. This is what God calls entering through the narrow gate. We are God's plan for all of creation. Christian believers are set aside for the special purposes of the Father.

In the New Testament, Jesus is the one, true way to the Father. God has chosen you as sons and daughters.

He has purposed your life to be a life in Him. His promises remain true and stand firm throughout all of life seasons. God promised a seed to come in Genesis; that seed was Jesus Christ our Savior. When Jesus died, God created a new covenant, a new promise (Matthew 26:28; Luke 22:19–20). God wants us as his servants and stewards to carry His Spirit within us. He has chosen us to be a light to show others the true way, the narrow gate.

You may be wondering how you can help the Lord carry this large plan out. It is easy. As Christian believers, your maturity in who God is deepens with reading of scripture and through fellowship and prayer. The Holy Spirit within you will also guide your way. You have to want the Father to use you. You have to be ready for your assignment as a believer. God wants to upgrade your walk with Him. Are you ready? Just being yourself, a believer in Jesus Christ, is the example for all to see. What you believe in your heart will reflect how you live your life. Others will see you in a new way and will want what you have. Now is your chance to give God all the glory for your transformation.

Share the good news with others. Tell them about your Father in heaven. Talk about your freedom in Christ and pray fervently with others. Lead them to Jesus. God's grace is infinite, and He has no boundaries. He has created in you a purpose to bring heaven here on earth. What are you waiting for? Praise Him and worship Him for all He has done for you. He loves you so much. He chose you. His son died for you to live to tell all who He is. He is wonderful, powerful, almighty, omnipresent, and omnipotent. His love for you will never fail. He is with you always. He is the One true way.

Behold! Humble yourself before the Lord; His spirit will guide you for the purpose of bringing others to Him.

About the Author

Michelle Gehrt is a former Outreach and Missions Director in Columbus, Ohio, where she started by serving the city and meeting the needs of the people in it. She has traveled the world as a short-term Missionary; bringing sustainable water systems and organizing a church build in the Dominican Republic. She is the wife to a wonderful husband, the mother of four grown children and three grandchildren. Michelle's early career was in the dental field, and after fifteen years, she changed in her scrubs after an impactful dental mission in Honduras. Her motto is Isaiah 6:8 "Here I am; send me." She lives her life as a vessel to be an example and a light for others to see. This is the first book that Michelle has written and has been prophetically activated from the heart of God and released through the Holy Spirit. Michelle has a heart for others and wants them to experience the Father's love the way she does. She has written this devotional to capture the hearts of others and win souls for Christ.

BIBLIOGRAPHY

The Modern Life Study Bible: God's Word for Our World
Copyright 2014 by Thomas Nelson, Inc. All rights
reserved.

Bible Commentary on line

Bible Gateway-https://www.Biblegateway.com/

Bible.org-https://Bible.org/

Biblehub.com-https://Biblehub.com/

Dictionary.com

Merriam Webster Dictionary on line

Oxford English Dictionary

CPSIA information can be obtained
at www.ICGtesting.com
Printed in the USA
LVHW022109260720
661578LV00016B/580